A Girl Named Trink

A Girl Named Trink

A Memoir of a Journey through Trauma and Healing

KATE RUBADUE

Serenity Ridge

A Girl Named Trink

A Memoir of a Journey through Trauma and Healing

Kate Rubadue

FIRST EDITION

ISBN: 978-0-578-46978-2

©2019 Kate Rubadue

Copyright. All rights reserved. Printed in the United States of America. No part of this book may be used or reproduced in any manner whatsoever without written permission except in the case of brief quotations embodied in critical articles and reviews.

Some names have been changed to protect the privacy of individuals.

Scripture passages are taken from the New International Version (NIV), New American Standard Bible (NASB), English Standard Version (ESV) and World English Bible (WEB), which are indicated after the verse quotations.

Dedicated to Michele, Rachel, and Jacqueline

«Introduction»

THIS IS MY STORY. In the coming pages I bare my soul, exposing my deepest secrets, weaknesses, brokenness, and private thoughts and feelings. I openly talk about taboo subjects, which may make the reader uncomfortable. It is not a natural part of our being to be open and transparent to others, let alone uncovering and reliving some of our most distressing memories. It leaves ourselves open to judgment and rejection.

Because of this, I debated whether or not to publish my memoir for fear of it causing damaging perceptions of my family and me.

After much soul searching, I decided to publish it because by being vulnerable, it can take one to a new place of connection and healing. One needs only to relate to one or more parts of my story to realize that my struggles, secrets, feelings of shame, and brokenness are similar to their own. By traveling along with me on my journey toward healing, my readers can heal as well.

My desire is to inspire and make a difference in the lives of others. It is my hope that my memoir will accomplish this purpose.

PART 1
Childhood

*"Dear Trink,
As much as you like to go out and play, remember that you as the eldest have a responsibility to your brothers and sister. We got you first, and want you to help.
Love, Dad"*

Written on a postcard addressed to me postmarked March, 1965 from Los Angeles, California when Dad was away on a business trip. I was ten years old.

«Chapter 1»

IT FELT LIKE A LONG TRIP to the hospital in Maryland. In fact it was a two-hour drive from our home in Falls Church, Virginia. I was nine years old. My younger sister, two brothers and I were in the back seat of our station wagon with my dad at the wheel. We were going to visit Mom. It had been over six months since we'd seen her. I longed to see her but I didn't know what to expect. I was sad that my mom had been away for so long. And during the time of her absence I had grown distant from her, afraid to be close to her again.

As we drove up the long stretch of road to the entrance of the building, Dad said we couldn't go inside. We were to wait outside on the lawn. He would get Mom and she would come out to meet us. I was in charge of watching over my sister and brothers while we waited.

I remember a tall, red brick building with lots of windows, but most of the blinds were closed. The building looked looming and uninviting. The grounds were large with lush green grass and big trees that provided lots of shade. It must have been springtime, but there was a chill in the air. I was wearing a dress with a sweater.

Then I saw a lady walking toward us with my dad trailing behind her. I was thinking, "Is that my mom? She's fat. My mom wasn't fat." She was crying but they weren't tears of joy. I remembered the crying. Mom used to cry a lot.

Liz, Mark, and Tony who was only three, ran into her arms. "Mommy, Mommy!" they cried with delight.

I didn't go toward her. Instead I walked away.

My mom called out, "Trinkie, you look so sad. Why do you walk away? Come give Mommy a hug."

I turned the other way, gazing downward. I made up my mind then and there. "That's not my mom and I don't love her. I never will."

I didn't know it then, but the hospital was a mental institution – Sheppard Pratt Hospital in Maryland. She was there for almost two years, from the time I was age nine to eleven.

My brother and sister recently told me that we eventually got to go inside the building in a meeting area for visitation with my mom.

"It was a spacious, sunlit room with floor-to-ceiling windows. There were other people in there. We visited her every fourth Sunday," Liz said.

I don't remember any of it. I guess I blocked it out.

«Chapter 2»

MY PARENTS WERE WELL EDUCATED. My dad, the youngest of three, received bachelor's and master's degrees from the University of California Santa Barbara (UCSB) and the University of California Los Angeles (UCLA) in electronics. My mother attended three years at the University of Southern California (USC) majoring in pharmacology. She was inspired by her dad who was a pharmacist and owned a store in Carpinteria, California, walking distance from the family home. Her mother worked the business side of things at the pharmacy.

Mom's parents divorced during her senior year at USC and she had to drop out to help take care of her five younger siblings while her mother took over the pharmacy, working full-time. Her father was never to be seen again. During her time at home, my mom attended a technical school and earned a degree in x-ray technology, and after moving out of the family home she worked as an x-ray technologist.

Born in Hollywood, Mom was raised both in Santa Barbara, California and the neighboring, coastal town of Carpinteria. Dad was born and raised in Carpinteria where his dad owned his own shop as an auto mechanic. The first cars my grandpa worked on were Model T Fords. Dad's mom was a stay-at-home mom, quite a bit younger than his dad.

Dad was an avid surfer, and the story Mom and Dad often told us kids is that they met on surfboards at Carpinteria State Beach and started dating soon afterward.

"I was 38-18-34 with a great tan," Mom would say.

"I married her for her figure," Dad would say, "and she was a virgin!" When he told me that as a child, I didn't know what that meant.

My mom was a beautiful woman, always with a big, white, toothy smile. Mom said Dad was so handsome he used to be mistaken for the movie star, Rock Hudson. Between my mom and my dad, she was the more sociable one. Dad was basically shy but when he drank, which would later become a problem, he came out of his shell and was often the life of the party. Dad was a very witty guy with a dry, cynical sense of humor.

Mom and Dad married in 1953 and bought their first home in Malibu, California. Dad was a World War II veteran who served in the Navy in the South Pacific, so he was able to purchase the home through the benefits of the G.I. bill. The G.I. bill provided low-cost mortgages, among other benefits, to World War II veterans. But Dad's financial benefits didn't end there. He had a rich uncle who died soon after Dad got married and left my dad a considerable amount of money. It provided my mom and dad a substantial nest egg, which apparently was invested well and lasted throughout my childhood. My siblings and I lived a very affluent and privileged lifestyle.

I was born in 1954 while my parents were still living in Malibu. My sister was born fourteen months later, although both of our birthplaces are actually Santa Monica. Dad entered the defense industry in electrical engineering and worked at a Navy base in Point Magu.

Three years later we moved to Acton, Massachusetts where my dad took an engineering job with Raytheon Corporation in Concord, a defense and aerospace company. After moving to Acton, my brother, Mark, was born in 1957.

During our time in Massachusetts, when I was three to four years old, is when my earliest memories began to form.

IT WAS CHRISTMAS MORNING. Liz and I walked down the stairs to see all the presents under the tree. I noticed a tricycle, which was for Liz, and a chalkboard desk with seats attached on each side. But I also noticed a child-size chair and red table with a blue and white phonograph on top, which had a large arm and record placed on the turntable. It was a phonograph made for kids, not like my dad's. I was immediately drawn to it. It was for me from Santa. My mother showed me how it worked. She helped me guide the arm with the needle over the record and it began to spin. Then came the music. It was classical music and I was entranced with all the different instrumental sounds, like the strings and the horns, and I especially loved the beautiful, interweaving melody, with the rise and fall of intensity. It moved me. I got lost in it. I understood it.

My mother later said that I was so absorbed she couldn't pull me away from the table to open my other presents. I just sat there and listened.

I still have those collections of records today – a set of five 45 rpms entitled "Leonard Bernstein's Young People's Concerts." They include Bach's Brandenburg Concerto No. 4, Brahms Symphony No. 2, Debussy, Copeland, Mussorgsky, and more.

My parents were both music enthusiasts although neither of them played an instrument. There was always music in the house. Mom and Dad would play records all day long – jazz, classical, Broadway, and movie soundtracks.

Now I had my own record player, and the music and I became one. I was four years old.

This was a happy time, as were the times Liz and I played in the snow that was taller than we were. The snow would be so frozen we could walk on top without falling through. In the summertime, we played in our yellow, inflatable swimming pool in the front yard with the girl from next door, and I would spray them with the hose. We swam in our underwear with our sunhats on. We drank out of cold, metal tumbler cups filled with homemade lemonade. Mom would chat with the other moms, sitting in lounge chairs watching us, laughing with us, drinking their lemonade too. Mom smiled a lot. She was doting and affectionate. She seemed happy.

«Chapter 3»

WHEN I WAS FOUR YEARS OLD we moved from Massachusetts back to California, this time to Camarillo. I don't remember much about that time except my first day of nursery school. I hated it. It was a big classroom with many rows of desks and lots of kids, and I started in the middle of the school year. I was extremely shy. I told my mom I never wanted to go back.

We only stayed in Camarillo for a year before we moved to Ann Arbor, Michigan where I started kindergarten. I remember our house and neighborhood vividly. Our house was a ranch style house and was newly built in a very nice suburban neighborhood. It wasn't even finished before we moved there and we lived in a hotel for what seemed like a week or so. I was five years old, Liz was four, and Mark was two. My school was behind our backyard separated by a chain link fence. I walked to school, usually escorted by my mom or an older student. I didn't like going to school there either. When our class would go out to the playground at recess time, I would sneak off and walk home. My mother would have to gather up Mark and Liz and walk me back. To keep me from running back home, my teacher finally had to hold my hand throughout recess. She tried to get me to play with the other kids but I didn't want to. I was so shy. But I remember liking art class.

I remember going on a field trip to a farm and I was fascinated with the dairy cows. The next day, the teacher asked the class to draw a picture about what interested us at the farm. I drew a cow, udders and all. My teacher found it humorous – drawing the udders. At the parent/teacher conference she showed off my artwork to my parents and said I was one of the best in the class. But more importantly, she told my parents that the only time I would really light up and smile was during music class, so much so that she recommended I take up playing an instrument.

We had a piano in the house at that time. Mom had decided to take piano lessons as an adult but didn't get very far. I was told that I would go up to the piano and with one or two fingers start picking out melodies on the keys. So after hearing what my kindergarten teacher said and knowing my love for music my parents found me a piano teacher, who also taught music at the University of Michigan, and I began piano lessons at age five. I still have my first lesson book which contains my first recital piece. My teacher said I definitely had musical talent. I loved playing the piano and even liked to practice, so much so that Mom and Dad never had to make me practice. I just loved to play and liked mastering a song, even at age five.

I was classically trained throughout my childhood and high school and I've been playing ever since. It has always been my outlet, my escape, and my therapy. I needed it as a child. Little did I know at age five how much I would need it as I grew older.

My mother said I was born shy. She said as a baby when she was holding me, if someone came up to me to "ooh and aah" over me I would bury my face in her bosom. Yes, I was painfully shy. But I also remember the nightmares when I was five and the way Dad responded to my fears, which didn't exactly give me a sense of security. I remember one instance in particular.

I saw a ghost in the closet, as plain as can be. I was on the top bunk, my sister on the bottom. In fear, I crawled into my parents' bed. My dad dragged me back into my bed. I still saw the ghost in the closet. I said, "Daddy, there's a ghost in the closet. He's staring at me."

Dad shouted angrily, "There's no ghost in the closet. Those are your white slips hanging in the closet. Go to sleep. Now!" He left the room but the ghost was still staring at me from the closet. I was so afraid that the ghost was going to come and get me that I lay awake watchfully, eyes wide opened.

I was afraid of my dad. He was intimidating. When I bring back my memories from age five, that's when I remember fearing him. That's when it started.

«Chapter 4»

WE MOVED AGAIN FROM Ann Arbor, Michigan to Falls Church, Virginia when I was six, entering first grade. Dad took a job with Bendix Corporation located in Washington D.C. as an aerospace engineer. He was moving up in the ranks. We lived in an upper class community called Lake Barcroft Estates. Our home was right on the lake with a large backyard surrounded by a thick forest. I remember as soon as we moved there, Dad enrolled us in swimming lessons so that we wouldn't drown in the lake. We had a row boat and my dad used to row us around the picturesque lake, exploring coves near the shore, and we'd admire the colorful Mallard ducks swimming around us. It was quiet and peaceful and the only ripples in the smooth, still water were from the boat, the oars, and the ducks.

I was enrolled in a private Catholic school called St. Anthony's. I remember having to wear a freshly pressed white blouse with a maroon, plaid uniform, a beanie and bow tie, and black and white saddle shoes which I had to polish every Sunday evening. My mother was a devout Catholic, having attended a private Catholic school from first to twelfth grade. My father was an atheist. According to Mom, she expressed to Dad that she'd marry him on the condition that their children would be raised in the Catholic faith. Dad agreed. Still, Dad never set foot in the church except when he was there for my First Communion and

Holy Confirmation (which he filmed with his 8 mm camera, tapes that I have to this day). It was Mom who took me, Liz, and Mark to Mass every Sunday.

Dad worked late hours and went on a lot of business trips. He was rarely home for dinner or even home for most of the week. But I do remember weekends where he would take the family for drives and picnics to places such as Gettysburg, Williamsburg, sites along the Potomac River, Great Falls, or to see the cherry blossoms in Washington D.C. during the spring. Dad loved the history of Virginia and the D.C. area and he made our trips educational. He'd read to us from all the plaques on the premises of the historic locations. I remember playing on the cannons at Gettysburg where Mark, Liz, and I would pretend to be in a battle. Dad would even play along.

Mom and Dad had a few good friends who they would entertain at our house, often having intellectual discussions or dancing the twist in our living room. My siblings and I would be downstairs playing with their kids, making a ruckus and having a ball. When Dad was traveling, Mom would hold down the fort busy being a mom. She enjoyed politics and even held the office of the president of the League of Women Voters.

My parents had it all together. They were a beautiful couple. Dad had a successful career and was a good provider. Mom was an affectionate, loving mother. We had a privileged life. But then a series of traumatic events followed, many leaving me scarred for the rest of my life.

«Chapter 5»

My aunt, who was a teenager at the time, was babysitting Liz, Mark, and me while Mom and Dad were out for the evening. I was six years old. Liz and I were in the basement, playing Superman with capes on, jumping off a table onto pillows placed on the floor. Once when I jumped, I missed the pillow, landed hard on the floor, and pain radiated through my lower leg and foot. I laid there on the floor screaming and crying. My aunt was upstairs and after hearing me she came down the stairs. She was irritated with all the carrying on I made and told me to stop crying like a baby and to get up and walk. I tried to but I couldn't. My leg felt limp. She then grabbed me by the arm, pulled me up the stairs while yelling at me, and dragged me to my bedroom.

Just then my parents came home during all the commotion. Once my aunt told them what had happened, Dad was mad that Liz and I were jumping off the table. I was afraid that he'd hit me, hurt leg or not. He didn't come into my room, but Mom was at my bedside tucking me in and told me I'd feel better in the morning. I do remember seeing concern on her face.

The next morning when it was time to dress and get ready for school, Mom came into the room and I told her I couldn't stand on my leg. She relayed it to Dad and he came in angry and told me that I was just trying to get out of going to school and that I was to get up and get dressed. I managed to dress myself while hopping on my good leg, but I struggled to put my shoe on my injured foot. Mom expressed to Dad again that I couldn't walk. Dad stood over me and said if I didn't stand on my leg he would hit me. Whenever Dad said he would hit any of us, we didn't argue. But I knew if I tried to put weight on my leg I would fall. I said in great fear, "I can't."

At that point Dad believed me, I think because he knew that if I were bold enough to challenge him then it must be real. He told Mom to take me to the emergency room.

The next thing I remember is being at the hospital and wheeled in for x-rays. Mom was there with me for a while but then left the room. She was gone quite a while and I wondered where she was and I wanted my mommy. The doctor was kind to me. He said I had broken my ankle and that I would need a cast. After some time went by he proceeded to put the cast on, but my mom didn't come back.

A friend of my mom's showed up at the hospital to take me home. Mom still wasn't around. I don't remember my mom's friend telling me what happened to her.

I found out much later that Mom had had a miscarriage. She was in her second trimester. I don't know if I even knew she was pregnant. They had admitted her to the hospital while I was getting the cast on my leg.

What was most traumatic for me about this experience was not just the fact that I had broken my leg and Mom wasn't there with me for the most part at the hospital, but how Dad threatened to hit me, not believing me. It wouldn't be the last time.

«Chapter 6»

WE HAD A MAID, MARGI, WHO worked for us part-time doing housework and caring for us. A lot of families in Lake Barcroft had maids, most of them black. Margi was half black and half American Indian. She was good to us. It wasn't just a luxury having her as I think Mom needed the help with Dad gone so much. Mom was also pregnant again and Margi was a help during her pregnancy. As I found out later, Mom had had four miscarriages between Mark's birth and this pregnancy. She was to take it easy. Apparently, her uterus ruptured when she had Liz and she was told never to have children again, but she got pregnant with Mark afterward and I guess there weren't any complications during that birth.

Then came Halloween of 1961. I was seven years old. Mom had gone into labor and she and Dad were at the hospital. Margi was home watching Liz, Mark, and me. While we were eating dinner, Margi told us a junk collector was coming to the house to collect some stuff out of our basement, and we were not to go down there. I disobeyed and went down to the basement out of curiosity. Margi was yelling at me, chasing after me down the stairs. I saw the junk collector about to carry a rusty, two-handed saw out of the basement. He told me to stay away. I didn't and tripped over the saw, cutting the front of my right leg open to the bone. I even saw the bone. Margi got all excited in a panic.

She grabbed a roll of gauze and wrapped my leg up tight, which was bleeding profusely.

Just then the phone rang and Margi answered. She said Mom just had the baby, a baby boy. Of course Margi didn't tell whoever it was what had happened to me.

Margi didn't drive so she didn't take me to the ER. But I guess she could have because a male friend of hers showed up to drive my siblings and me around for Halloween to trick-or-treat. So there was a driver, but for some reason taking me to the ER wasn't their priority, even though I had a gash in my leg cut to the bone. I remember my siblings and me sitting in the backseat of the car with the man driving and Margi on the passenger side. They stopped at each house and let Mark and Liz out of the car to trick-or-treat with their pillow cases and an extra one for me.

"Our sister is in the car with a hurt leg and she can't walk. Could you please give us extra candy for her?" And the people at the door did.

The next day my mom's best friend, Mrs. O'Connor, took me to the doctor's office. I needed stitches and they wanted to give me a shot of Novocain beforehand. I was deathly afraid of needles and refused to have the shot. "If that's the way you want it," the doctor said.

I was lying down on the table and Mrs. O'Connor was at my side holding my hand. When the doctor started the poking to stitch me up, I cried bloody murder and thrashed about. The doctor called in an army of nurses and they all held me down. "I want my mommy!" I cried. "I want my mommy!"

Mrs. O'Connor said, "Your mommy is in the hospital with your new baby brother. She can't be here. Be a big girl."

I was mad and upset. With all the nurses holding me down, I got the stitches.

Later, I found out that Mom almost died giving birth to my brother, Tony. Her uterus ruptured again and she almost bled to death. At that time, fathers weren't usually allowed in the birthing room, but when the doctors didn't think my mom would make it they called my dad in and a priest to administer last rites to her.

Mom ended up getting a total hysterectomy. I say total because in those days they took out everything – ovaries and all. My mom was both physically and emotionally traumatized with her hormones going haywire. Mom also wanted more children and having a hysterectomy was devastating to her. She was only thirty-one years of age.

Her serious physical condition didn't end there. Three days after the hysterectomy both her kidneys shut down. She had to have immediate surgery to remove one of them. I assume she was on dialysis for a while. She was in the hospital for months.

My new baby brother, Tony, came home soon after his birth and Margi was there full-time taking care of him and us. However, since she wasn't at our home twenty-four hours a day, seven days a week, my sister and I, ages six and seven, had to help take care of Tony. We changed his diapers (and those were the days of cloth diapers and safety pins), bottle fed him, rocked him, put him to bed, and washed out his poopy diapers in the toilet … all the things you do for a baby.

We finally got to visit Mom at the hospital. I'm not sure how much time had passed after Tony's birth. But I remember the visit vividly.

There was a courtyard in the center of the hospital. Dad led us through the courtyard to Mom's room. I remember how white and sterile everything was. Mom was sitting up and actually smiling. She was so glad to see us.

Dad had told me beforehand, "Don't tell Mom about what happened to your leg."

Well, I didn't obey. When I walked up to Mom, the first thing I did was whisper to her what happened to my leg. I yearned for Mommy's comfort when it happened and I yearned for Mommy then. I should have known better. Mom was troubled by what I said and told my dad. Dad later got really angry with me and I felt guilty and frightened.

After what seemed like a long time, Mom finally came home. Selfish as it may sound, I finally had my mom back.

«Chapter 7»

AFTER LIVING IN OUR FIRST home in Lake Barcroft for a year, in 1961 we moved to another area of the lake which was even more beautiful than the last and located near the dam. Our house was a brand new, large two-story house situated on top of a hill which descended down to the lake. It was surrounded by wooded empty lots which included cypress trees, pine trees, dogwoods, willow trees, and blackberry and honeysuckle bushes. I often played in the woods, picking blackberries and licking the honey off the honeysuckles. I was a tomboy and I would make believe I was an Indian or Huckleberry Finn and I'd carry a knapsack on the end of a stick as I'd explore trails. I would dig for worms which I used for fishing off the dock that my dad built.

We had a boat as most families living on the lake had. They included sailboats and "party barges". No motorboats were allowed on the lake so the water was usually calm and peaceful. There were five private beaches for swimming with lifeguard stands and the beaches were named "Beach 1", "Beach 2", "Beach 3", and so on. My siblings, friends, and I would often swim or sail across the lake to Beach 4, which was across the lake from our property. We were all good swimmers. During the summertime, we spent most every day in the water.

Lake Barcroft Estates offered many summer activities for kids and adults alike, including sailboat racing, swimming lessons, and a Labor Day festival called the "Beach Olympics," featuring a parade of floats made and decorated by the children. A Teen Queen and her court were part of the parade, waving at us on shore from their floats. They were so pretty. I remember thinking, "I want to be a queen someday."

There were beach games like the "penny pile" where pennies and the prize silver dollars were hidden in a huge sand pile that the kids would dig for after hearing "Ready! Set! Go!" There were sack races and three-legged races. In the winter the lake would freeze over and we would ice skate just off the shore of our own backyard. We'd play "Crack the Whip" where the kids would form a line holding hands with the "head" of the whip leading us in random directions. I liked being at the tail, being whipped across the ice faster than anyone else.

Lake Barcroft Estates, developed in the 1950s, attained upscale status in the beginning of the 1960s. Notable politicians such as President Kennedy's press secretary, Pierre Salinger, and Attorney General Ramsey Clark moved into the community, as did many other senators and congressmen. In fact our next door neighbor was Pierre Salinger. I remember that our bus stop was at the end of his driveway and as we were waiting for the bus, Pierre Salinger's large, black limousine would pick him up to take him to the White House during John F. Kennedy's presidency. Once or twice President Kennedy himself would visit Mr. Salinger at his home and we would peek through the woods from our backyard to try to get a good look at him lounging by the lake.

Dad used to say to us, "You are privileged to live in such a nice house and neighborhood. Be appreciative. Not everyone lives like this." I don't think I fully understood it at the time.

Dad loved the water. He was in heaven living on the lake and going out on the boat. But even more so, he loved the ocean. Not surprising since he grew up in the coastal town of Carpinteria and surfed as a boy at the Rincon, a popular surfing spot. However, there weren't many surfers during those days in the 1950s. Dad was one of the pioneers. Several times he told us that he surfed with the actor Peter Lawford at the Rincon. They would surf on the heavy, long surfboards made out of fiberglass and polyurethane foam. Dad used to make his own. In fact, Dad told us that back then he had dreams of opening his own surf shop selling boards and just wanted to be a surf bum. In his later years Dad would tell us, "I should have opened that shop. I'd be making millions today."

Having a family and an executive career in aerospace didn't stop him from surfing. We spent many spring breaks and summers at Virginia Beach, about a four-hour drive each way from our home in Lake Barcroft. Dad used to call himself "the executive surfer". We'd spend a week or so at a motel along the boardwalk and Dad would get up at dawn and catch a few waves.

"Surf's up!" he'd say.

Then Mom and we kids would later join him on the beach, body surfing, playing in the sand making drip sand castles, digging up sand crabs and collecting shells, including beautiful large-sized conch shells. Dad would even take me out in the water and stand me up on his board and give me a push to catch a wave. I'd ride it all the way in. It wasn't hard because the board was as heavy and sturdy as a boat and I was as light as a feather. But I remember the other surfers frantically getting out of my way as I plowed through the water into shore, not knowing how to steer.

The whole family loved the beach and ocean almost as much as Dad did. But we used to get so sunburned. Before Coppertone sunscreen came out, Dad would line us up and baste us in vegetable oil with a basting brush. I guess he thought it would reflect the sun. Well needless to say we were burnt to a crisp. I remember Mom would rub Noxzema lavishly all over our bodies for soothing, which didn't work at all, and we'd be moaning in pain. I tanned easier than my siblings, so I didn't burn as bad. But it didn't bode well for getting different forms of skin cancer in our later years.

Despite the sunburns, those were good times.

«Chapter 8»

I WAS SEVEN YEARS OLD and had been taking piano lessons for about a year from a sweet, elderly lady whose name was Mrs. Ashley. She taught from a studio in Arlington, Virginia. I liked her very much. Like the first teacher I had in Michigan, she said I had a lot of talent. I started playing simple classical pieces at that time. I performed in my first recital when I was seven in front of a large audience. I was petrified, but I did well. Mom and Dad eventually became friends with Mr. and Mrs. Ashley and they would occasionally come to our house to visit.

Dad would drop me off at the studio and pick me up when my lesson was over. On one occasion, I was sitting in the waiting room by myself waiting for Mrs. Ashley to come get me for my lesson. Soon I noticed Mr. Ashley walking through the door sobbing and he went over to some ladies at the reception desk who worked there. He talked to them in a hushed tone but I heard what he said. Mrs. Ashley had died. They looked over at me knowing that I was waiting for my lesson with her. They didn't tell me that she had died. One of the ladies went out of the room and after a while came back with a young man with a friendly smile. She said I would be taking lessons from him that day. So I followed him to the back room and took my piano lesson, but I was sad. I didn't mention to him what I knew, and he didn't say anything to me either.

After my lesson was over, Dad picked me up. When we rode in the car we were both very quiet. Then I turned to him and said, "Daddy, Mrs. Ashley died."

Seeing the expression on his face, it looked like he was hearing it for the first time. But he didn't show emotion. Then he said to me, "Let's go get ice cream."

That was one of the tender moments I remember with my dad. He didn't express his feelings much. Suggesting we get ice cream was the closest he got to showing his caring and affection.

«Chapter 9»

DAD WOULD TAKE US ON many Sunday drives to the historic parts of D.C. and Virginia. On this particular day, we were going to have a picnic along the Potomac River. We all piled into the station wagon and headed out to the river on a bright, sunny day.

Just as we set off Mom asked, "Kenny, did you make sure the oven is off? Is the iron off? Is the stove off? Did you remember to bring Tony's bottles?"

"Yes, dear," Dad said.

She'd ask these questions every time we'd start off on a trip.

I loved our Sunday drives and the picnics. I was looking forward to this day. After we arrived at the park along the river, Mom spread out the red and white checkered tablecloth on the picnic table and unpacked the picnic basket full of homemade fried chicken and potato salad, chips and onion dip and watermelon, and Dad brought the cooler full of sodas and beer for himself.

"Kids, you can go play until we're ready to eat, but don't go near the water!" Mom said.

There were swans swimming just off the riverbank and butterflies fluttering about, which I tried to catch. My brother Mark had his plastic baseball bat and whiffle ball and we played ball. I skipped rocks across the water, and I was pretty good at it, and Mark, Liz, and I just laughed and played. Mom was bottle-feeding Tony. After a while we were called in to eat.

We were just taking our first few bites when Mom started crying in a panic. "We have to go! The voices … the people. We have to go!"

I'm looking about thinking, "What's happening? What voices? What people?"

Mom became hysterical. She insisted we pack up and go home. And so we did.

I didn't know it then, but she was having an anxiety attack, and many were to follow

MY SIBLINGS AND I WERE at Mass with Mom sitting in one of the center pews. Mom was all dressed up pretty with her black veil pinned on top of her head, as was mine. Mark and Liz were squirming about in the pew, as kids often do in church. I sat quietly and attentively. The Mass was spoken in Latin in those days but I knew the responses having learned them in religion class; plus we had our missal book to read from.

Mass was about halfway through when Mom was in a panic again. She stood up and told us we had to go. She abruptly gathered us up and walked us out of the church. I was embarrassed. We went to the car and when she sat down behind the wheel she started crying hysterically. She just cried and cried. How she drove us home, I don't know.

She never took us to Mass again. Dad would make sure we still attended, though. He would drop us off and pick us up, still resistant to set foot in the church.

MOM'S ANXIETY ATTACKS got worse. They became a daily occurrence at home. She would not only get in a panic state, acting like she was seeing and hearing things with great trepidation, but she would constantly vomit in the toilet. I'd hear it every day – that along with her constant crying. She also developed agoraphobia. To quote a definition by the Mayo Clinic:

> *"Agoraphobia is a type of anxiety disorder in which you fear and avoid places or situations that might cause you to panic and make you feel trapped, helpless or embarrassed. You fear an actual or anticipated situation, such as using public transportation, being in open or enclosed spaces, standing in line, or being in a crowd.*
> *The anxiety is caused by fear that there's no easy way to escape or get help if the anxiety intensifies. Most people who have agoraphobia develop it after having one or more panic attacks, causing them to worry about having another attack and avoid the places where it may happen again."*

Mom could no longer drive or set foot outside the front door. At one point, she got where she couldn't leave her bedroom.

LIZ AND I WERE IN THE living room and Mom ran out of her room. "Tie me up! Tie me up so I don't kill you!" Mom cried.

I ran out of the house. Liz stayed behind, as she always did. Liz would stay to take care of Mom. I would run away.

MOM BEGAN SEEING a psychiatrist. She had a friend who would drive her to her appointments weekly. The doctor's name was Dr. Morris. She was very fond of him. But she wasn't getting better. I'm guessing she saw him for about two years. Then one day, as I learned later, this happened:

Mom was in the waiting room waiting for her appointment. Time was ticking by and it got past her appointment time and Dr. Morris still hadn't come out of his office. After waiting a long time, she knocked on his door and after getting no response, she opened it. She found him collapsed on the floor.

As it turned out, he had a massive heart attack. He was only in his early thirties. He survived, but during his recovery Mom was referred to another psychiatrist. It didn't go well. After the loss of Dr. Morris as her doctor, she fell apart. She had a nervous breakdown. Soon afterward, her new doctor committed her to a mental institution – Sheppard Pratt in Maryland. She was diagnosed with severe anxiety disorder and borderline psychosis.

I was nine years old and in fourth grade when she was committed. But all I knew was that she was in a hospital. No one told me why.

«Chapter 10»

AFTER MOM WAS COMMITTED, Dad needed to find full-time care for the four of us. So he began a search for a maid who would act as our nanny as well as do the cooking and cleaning. We went through a series of them, all black. Some would last just a week. "They're too unruly," one would say.

After a certain trial time, for those who didn't quit, Dad would sit us down and ask if we liked them. There were some we didn't like at all. Dad listened and then tried out another one.

Chris came along. We liked her very much. Dad hired her and she stayed on permanently. She lived with us during the week, day and night, having her own small room downstairs. During the weekends she lived in her home in Washington D.C. with her mother who was blind. She wasn't married and had no kids of her own. Dad was usually home during the weekends to look after us, after continuing to go on business trips during most of the week. That didn't absolve Liz and me of our duties though. We were still changing Tony's diapers.

One time I didn't rinse out a soiled diaper in the toilet and just threw it in the hamper. Dad found out. He came to me with the poopy diaper in hand, fuming. "Trink, you didn't clean out this diaper did you … did you?" he yelled.

"No," I said in trepidation.

He hit me in the head with his bare hand and sent me to my room, which was downstairs, by kicking me down the stairs. I wet my pants. He did that a lot – kicking us down the stairs when we were in trouble, except for my baby brother. Whether it was only one of us who misbehaved or all three of us, he'd drag us to the top of the stairs, grab our heads, and bang them together like the Three Stooges. Then one by one he would lift us up by the scruff of our collar, give us a swift kick in the pants, let go, and we went tumbling down the stairs. (Remarkably, there were no broken bones). I didn't cry though. I was scared that it would just make him madder. In fact, I hardly ever showed emotion around my dad. My siblings responded the same way. We all lived in great fear of him.

Chris was strict but not in a bad way. She smiled and laughed readily but she wasn't affectionate with us. For example, I never remember her hugging us; sitting us in her lap reading a bedtime story; tucking us in at night; or consoling us when we cried after scraping a knee or getting stung by a bee. She took care of our basic needs but she didn't go much beyond that. However, I remember her dancing jubilantly with Tony when he was a toddler to the tune of Louis Armstrong singing "Hello Dolly" on the radio. She loved Louis Armstrong. She got a kick out of Tony swinging to the rhythm, laughing in glee.

Chris didn't drive but she took us for walks. One day she walked us to an ice cream store near our neighborhood called Gifford's. She gave us each some change. When we reached the store and started to go inside, she wasn't coming in with us. She stood outside the door. "Chris, why aren't you coming in?" I asked.

She frowned and looked out in the distance, shaking her head no.

"Come on Chris. Don't you want some ice cream?"

She didn't answer. So I went on in and my siblings and I bought our ice cream cones.

I later found out that she couldn't go in because she was black. It was an all-white store, as were all the stores and restaurants around us – the grocery store, drug store, cleaners, jewelry store ... those were the days of segregation. If you were black, you had to go to your own stores, which I never saw. Schools were segregated too. Black people couldn't even share water fountains or restrooms with the whites.

My parents were not prejudiced and my father treated Chris very well. My parents, being from California where few blacks lived, didn't understand the prejudice. But it was all around us. Our neighbor across the street was a true southerner with deep prejudice; so much so that he disapproved of Chris living in our house.

On Friday nights, Dad would drive Chris back to her apartment in Washington D.C. with my brothers, sister, and me riding in the back seat of the car. She lived in a bad part of town. I remember as we rode in our Cadillac on the street near her house, young black kids would throw stones at us. They would do it every time we'd drive by them. Chris spoke to them later and told them we were good people and not to throw rocks. So they stopped.

We would often go inside her apartment to visit for a while. It was a small two-story place. One day she took me upstairs to her bedroom and showed me the dolls on her bed. They were black. I didn't know they made black dolls. I thought all dolls were white. I told Chris that. "Blacks are people too," she said.

Chris's words to me, and seeing dolls that were black, made a big impression on me.

«Chapter 11»

AFTER MOM WENT INTO THE hospital, Dad started drinking heavily, beers and martinis. Dad got more unpredictable, mean, and wild. He would do random things like throw a batch of freshly baked cookies out the backdoor and declare, "That was for nothing, so you better watch out!" That was one of his favorite lines. He had lots of lines. He'd tell us "Shape up or ship out!" He'd call us "Dumb toots" and called me "Hose nose". I don't know why because I didn't have a big nose, but he made me think I did.

Another favorite saying of his was, "Do as I say, not as I do." If it was a Thursday, he'd ask "What day is it?" I'd answer, "Thursday." He'd toast a drink in his hand and say, "Thursday? Don't mind if I do!" (He made "Thursday" synonymous with "thirsty"). He'd randomly grab our cheeks with one hand so that our lips were pursed. "Say Buttermouth Perch," he'd say. "Buttermouth Perch," we'd respond. He'd bellow, "Ha ha ha!" and we'd crack a smile like it was funny.

More of his favorite sayings were: "Stick it in your ear;" "Only in America;" "Write if you get work;" "Close but no cigar;" "You can't hit the ground with your hat;" "Holy tamolies;" "That's a bunch of malarkey;" "I'll drink to that." If I asked him what a word meant he'd say, "Look it up in your funken wagnel, it's the only way you'll learn."

The first Christmas holiday without our mom home we were decorating the Christmas tree. I placed the tinsel on neatly to make it look real pretty and showed it to Dad. He stood back, looked at the tree and said, "Take it all off. You aren't supposed to put it on neatly. You're supposed to throw it on." So we all had to take the tinsel off and throw it back on. "Now that's the way you're supposed to do it," he said.

The music on the record player got louder and louder. He would open all the windows so the neighbors could hear. He'd play his favorite record over and over again. One of them was by a group of Irish musicians called "The Irish Rovers". Dad played it full blast, getting drunker and drunker. He said he had Irish blood in him and so it was an excuse for him to drink (based on the belief that the Irish like to drink). Thus, St. Patrick's Day was one of his favorite holidays, a day in which he would always get sloshed. He loved to party on any holiday actually. So I came to dread the holidays when he was around because that's when he drank the most. I would be on my best behavior.

People thought Dad was funny. He was a very eccentric man, a real character, had quick wit, and was always the life of the party. Sometimes I *did* think he was funny, as long as I wasn't the brunt of it.

I always thought Dad was a genius. I still think my dad was a genius. I was told his IQ was over 140. He was a top executive in his field and very respected. At the time, he worked on a missile program and now and then he brought home models of missiles. I was so thrilled when he gave me one to keep. I remember times he would help me with my homework when he hadn't been drinking. He taught me how to study using the SQ3R method – survey, question, read, recite, and review. Those moments were special to me because it was one of the few times I felt real tenderness from him. It was important to my dad for my siblings and me to get a good education. He urged all of us to go to college, and in our adulthood all four of us earned college degrees.

There were other tender moments when Dad showed me he really cared. One time I was about nine years old and had just finished watching a movie by myself starring Doris Day about a boy who was kidnapped and separated from his mother. I remember throughout the movie the boy screaming, "I want my mommy!" It made me so scared that I wanted to go to my dad and climb in his bed, and I wanted my mommy. I feared my dad, but I was more scared to be by myself at that moment. So I went to Dad's room and told him I was scared and I missed Mommy. I asked him if I could lie in his bed. He looked sympathetic. He said yes.

Dad was a dichotomy to me. It was like he had a dual personality. I feared him and I admired him. I loved him and I hated him. I couldn't reconcile the image of a handsome, educated, smart, engineering professional and sometimes tender man with the monster that he could be.

IT WAS EASTER AND DAD took us kids to Virginia Beach for Easter break. We stayed at a motel. Dad had a lady with him. He and she stayed in one room and we stayed in the neighboring room. I was to babysit my siblings. I was about ten years old. I didn't quite understand who the lady was. The day before Easter, Dad took me to a store and asked me to pick out Easter baskets for Liz, Mark, and Tony. They still believed in the Easter bunny, or at least Mark and Tony did.

I remember thinking, "I'm not supposed to do this. I'm a child too. I'm still a little girl. Who gets me *my* Easter basket?"

Many times Dad took home movies with his 8 mm camera. As an adult, I watched this particular home movie of our vacation to Virginia Beach at Eastertime and that lady was in the movie. She was a very attractive lady with a good figure shown in a bathing suit on the beach. I asked my sister, "Who was that lady?"

She answered, "That was his mistress. She was one of many."

«Chapter 12»

Dad told us, "Mom is coming home to spend the day with us."

My siblings and I were all excited, even though I had decided I didn't love her anymore. Dad picked Mom up from the hospital, and when we heard him pull into our driveway, all of us stood in the kitchen with Chris in anticipation. Mom walked through the door with Dad behind her. We started to run to her to hug her. Then she broke down and cried. She had another panic attack. She was barely in the door when she told Dad to take her back. She didn't stay. Dad took her back to the hospital. I was devastated.

Mom eventually came home for good when I was in sixth grade, eleven years old. Two years previous, when Mom was committed, she still had her good figure, even after four kids. She was 5'2" and slender but buxomly with a small waist and curvy hips. When she came home from the hospital, she weighed over 200 pounds. It was the medication that caused the weight gain. As far as medication, she was taking everything under the sun – tranquilizers, pills to wake up, pills to go to sleep … you name it. When she carried her purse around, it would rattle from all the bottles of pills she carried in it.

When Mom began to have an anxiety attack, still almost an everyday occurrence, she'd pop a pill to sedate herself. She would take more than prescribed and was becoming a prescription drug addict. She still couldn't drive and didn't leave the house, and Chris continued to care for us because Mom was unable to do so. Mom still cried. She'd cry and cry all day long. I hated it and I hated her. I became callous and apathetic toward her. I wanted nothing to do with her.

When she cried and carried on, she'd say, "Come to Mommy. Give Mommy a hug."

I felt like she needed us to mother her and was not mothering us. I resented it. My brothers and sister would give her the hugs she wanted. I would run out of the room.

Dr. Morris was back in practice and Mom went back to seeing him. She was more than fond of him, she was infatuated with him. Even though he was her age, I think she saw him as a father figure. They call it transference.

Then came the day Dad announced, "We're moving. We're moving to Michigan." Dad was still with Bendix Corporation and had accepted a promotion.

Mom was upset with the news. "I can't leave Dr. Morris," she said. Chris wasn't happy either. She had been with us for five years. She loved our family. *She was part of our family*. She couldn't imagine us leaving, and I couldn't imagine us leaving her either. But we did.

«Chapter 13»

We moved to an upscale neighborhood in Pontiac, Michigan. I was enrolled in a public school called "Bloomfield Hills Junior High". I was entering seventh grade. I had been going to a private Catholic school in Virginia from grades one through six so this was a big change for me, not to mention moving to a new state and entering junior high. We moved into a very large, stately, two-story white house. It was nestled in the woods near a lake and was very beautiful. We moved there in the summertime and I remember water skiing on the lake for the first time. I also made new friends right away in the neighborhood. But when I started school I was so very shy. Doing well in academics became more important to me. It meant everything to me to get straight A's to the point of obsession. If I got a B+ I would chastise and belittle myself. I think academics offered me stability in my unstable surroundings and also self-esteem when I did get the A's. I also continued to take piano lessons and playing the piano offered me solace.

Mom had more anxiety attacks. The first week we moved to Pontiac, I came home from a friend's house to find a neighbor sitting next to Mom in our family room, consoling her while she was crying in hysteria. The lady said to me, "Your mom is sick."

I think she thought my mom was physically ill. I gave her a dirty look and went upstairs to my room. I was disgusted with my mom. The lady had a look of surprise and disapproval.

WE ONLY LIVED IN PONTIAC, MICHIGAN for nine months before moving to Cocoa Beach, Florida in mid-March, 1967. Dad accepted a job as vice president with Bendix Corporation to work on the Apollo space program. Dad managed a staff from his own office near Cape Canaveral and worked with the astronauts. (The Apollo program, which ran from 1961 to 1972, was carried out by NASA with the goal of landing the first man on the moon. The program succeeded in reaching its goal. A total of twelve American astronauts walked on the moon. The first landing took place on July 20, 1969 and the last in December, 1972).

Our family was privileged to watch the launches. Since it was so flat in Florida, we could easily view the take-offs from our front yard, and when we were in school the students were let out to watch the launches from the parking lot. I especially liked viewing the launches at night because you could see the three stages take place. In the first stage, the boosters detach from the rest of the rocket leaving a smaller rocket; in the second stage, the rocket fires and separates leaving an even smaller rocket; in the third stage, the rocket ignites before separation and is thrust into space. We'd see small explosions at each stage in the night sky. It was quite a sight. When Saturn V was launched, the notable television broadcast journalist Walter Cronkite was there to broadcast it and my dad and mom dined with him in the dining room on the NASA base.

We lived only two blocks from the beach which we all took pleasure in and Dad continued to surf. Our house was right on a canal and we had our own private dock. We had a 28-foot motorboat and after that a 26-foot sailboat. As a family we used to take one-or-two-week-long boat trips in the canal and the Indian River, which emptied out into the Atlantic, cruising up and down the Atlantic coast. Living on the canal was like a scene out of the T.V. show "Flipper" where dolphins would actually swim up to our dock. I also fished off of it and mostly caught catfish.

I played with my friends swinging off a rope, which was tied to a tree, into the water. We went canoeing, had tree forts, secret clubs, played at the recreational center on the trampoline, played street football – I was still a tomboy, and did all the things kids do, mostly playing outdoors. Mom couldn't stand the mugginess and the bugs, especially the mosquitoes and chiggers. We always had "Off" sprayed all over us whenever we were outside and smelled of it, too. As kids we didn't mind too much but I can understand why my mom didn't like it.

While living in Cocoa Beach, I attended Roosevelt Junior High and Cocoa Beach High school from seventh to tenth grade. I experienced typical peer pressure and insecurities at school and had an obsession with getting good grades.

Mom continued to have her anxiety attacks, abused her medication, and rarely drove. She saw a psychiatrist while we lived there. Dad continued to drink and was getting worse.

After the launch of Apollo 13, Dad was taken off the program. I'm not sure of the reasons, but it meant that Dad had to find a new job. He was offered a job in Alabama. We were going to move there and my dad actually purchased a house there, but we ended up moving back to Falls Church, Virginia during the summer of 1970. Dad was able to stay with Bendix.

«Chapter 14»

I was given a diary as a gift for my twelfth birthday from my parents. It was one of those lock and key diaries called, "A Line a Day Five Year Diary". I wrote in it religiously every day and it was my friend. My first entry was on my twelfth birthday on September 3, 1966, and my last entry was March 1, 1970, when I was fifteen. It is a treasure trove of firsthand information of me as a young girl entering her adolescent years, writing about typical emotional changes that happen during puberty. For example, wanting to be popular in school and dealing with peer pressure, having crushes on boys and being noticed, having mood swings and feeling self-conscious about myself. But then there are the experiences and feelings I wrote about which resulted from growing up in a dysfunctional family, feelings that aren't typical of an adolescent growing up in a stable, loving environment.

In the following pages, I have included excerpts of my diary so that the reader can experience vicariously the tumultuous emotions I suffered through and the events that happened while living in Pontiac, Michigan, and Cocoa Beach, Florida. My last diary entry ends just before the move back to Virginia.

Diary entries

September 7, 1966: First day of school. Did so much walking and terrible lunch. I'm mad at Mom. She is getting mad at everybody.

September 8, 1966: A hard day at school. People are making fun of me because I don't wear nylons. I wear socks.

September 15, 1966: Got braces on my upper teeth. They're killing me.

September 30, 1966: I'm getting my report card this month so I better shape up or ship out.

October 6, 1966: The school counselor called Mom and said to her I'm a serious child.

October 15, 1966: We went to a drive-in movie. First one was love stuff.

October 26, 1966: I keep getting balled out for getting mad at Mommy, every day. Mommy's really mad at me.

November 6, 1966: I'm mad at everybody. EVERYBODY'S AGAINST ME!

November 22, 1966: I still have the feeling that Mommy blames everything on me. I'm sick of her!

November 29, 1966: There's a cute boy named Dan. He's in 9th grade but I like him and he doesn't know it. He gave me gum today and nobody else.

December 15, 1966: I'm mad at Mommy. She always gets mad at me and blames me. I wish I had nerve to run away!

December 16, 1966: Still mad at Mommy. In gym, teacher was getting personal about LIFE!

December 19, 1966: Mad at Mommy. Got B+ in Spanish. Wanted to get A+. About to cry!

December 20, 1966: A boy came and walked with me and said he loved me. Didn't pay attention to him.

January 4, 1967: Saw 3 films in school. Home Ec. Film about girls! Mom's mad again. I almost hate her.

January 6, 1967: Wasn't my day today. Daddy was mad.

January 12, 1967: Mommy and Daddy had a fight. Aunt Teri was going to come here this Monday to help Mommy, but now she isn't.

January 18, 1967: The boy who came up to me and said I love you said it to me again. Found out his name. It's Greg.

February 3, 1967: Got our report cards today and I got six A's and two B's!

February 12, 1967: Daddy left for Florida.

February 14, 1967: Only got Valentine's cards from Lizzie, Mark, and Tony!

February 18, 1967: Daddy came back from Florida and he wants to move!

March 3, 1967: We might move to Florida and I hope we do cause I really want to.

March 7, 1967: Dad said we're moving to Florida and I'm so happy!

March 11, 1967: Grandma is coming to Florida with us and she came today. I'm so excited.

March 14, 1967: I got out of school during sixth period because we are moving right away. I cried because I missed everybody.

March 27, 1967: We're in Cocoa Beach, our new homeland. We're in a motel. It's right by the ocean.

April 1, 1967: Went to school and wore white socks and people made fun of me. I'm really mad at Mom today.

April 3, 1967: Went to school and I'm so scared or something like wishing it was my other school.

April 5, 1967: We had an assembly at school. I'm riding the bus now. I'm getting shyer every minute.

April 18, 1967: I hate myself! I can't do anything right. Everyone mad at me and I strike out all the time in baseball.

April 23, 1967: I didn't feel very good today. I just sat around the house getting yelled at all the time.

April 25, 1967: After school I went for a walk in the woods. I didn't feel good because of school. I wanted to be alone.

April 26, 1967: I wish I were dead! No one loves or likes me. Everyone makes fun of me. I don't see what's wrong with me!

May 2, 1967: I'M SO STUPID! I didn't speak to my friends because I was unhappy about the grade on my history test. I hate myself.

June 11, 1967: Daddy's birthday. We stayed up till four last night. I almost fell asleep in church. I slept when I came home.

June 12, 1967: We went to the beach today. I got a nice tan. Then I went fishing when we got home. I caught 3 catfish.

June 26, 1967: We got a new boat called "Suzy Q". It's real big with a stove and icebox and beds ...

August 7, 1967: We went to the beach and Dad and I went surfing on the same surfboard at the same time.

October 16, 1967: I got my report card and got straight A's! I'm so happy I can't believe it.

October 17, 1967: Everyone was yelling at me today. I'm in a bad mood. I HATE everyone.

October 18, 1967: Today was OK I guess. I didn't do much except do a whole bunch of tests and probably got D's and F's.

October 19, 1967: Well it didn't turn out D's and F's. I got A's on all my tests. I was so worried.

November 16, 1967: I got a B+ on my English test. I'm so upset. I can't do anything right anymore.

January 26, 1968: We went out to dinner at an Italian Restaurant. Mom got a little scared.

March 4, 1968: Stayed after school to play football. It's lots more fun to play with boys.

March 8, 1968: Went to beach and the water was freezing. I went surfing with Daddy.

March 11, 1968: My Spanish teacher said I'm the best student anyone could have. I'm happy. If you ask me I think I'm smart.

April 16, 1968: I snuck in Lizzie's diary and all she puts on every page is "I love Mommy." She's a queer.

May 6, 1968: Every time Daddy goes on a trip my mother yells at me. I bet she's afraid when Daddy's around.

May 7, 1968: My mom is mean to me. I swear, Lizzie's her pet. I wish she loved me. I might run away!

May 19, 1968: I ran away today. My mother slapped me for no reason. I went out my window. I went down to a secret place and cried. They found me.

June 6, 1968: Senator Robert Kennedy got shot three times. One in the head, very critical. It's sad. Also hurricane Abby is coming.

June 7, 1968: Robert Kennedy died. It's so sad.

July 25, 1968: I got hit so hard today by Dad, I almost got knocked out. I hate everyone! My family's full of HELL!

August 9, 1968: Daddy came home from trip and got in fight with Mom.

August 27, 1968: Boy! I'm so scared when I go to piano lessons. I'm afraid my teacher will hit me for doing something wrong.

September 11, 1968: Went to orthodontist and get my braces off this Monday! I'm so excited! Plucked my eyebrows and look terrible!

November 4, 1968: Love P.E. now cause we're playing football and I'm good! (For a girl).

November 10, 1968: Didn't go to church today since Daddy's in Puerto Rico and we have no one to take us.

November 16, 1968: Didn't sleep a wink last night. Also threw up again. Mom took care of me and slept with me.

December 5, 1968: MY MOM IS A *$&%*()@&! I'm going to run away! I hate the whole world and God for making me GROSS!

December 12, 1968: Lizzie received confirmation and Mark sang in the choir. Mom, Tony, and I didn't go. Mom didn't feel up to it.

December 13, 1968: My Mom is a damn *#@%* queer and a gross pig! I hate her. I hate myself for living. God's mean.

December 17, 1968: Lizzie's birthday. She's only in 7th grade and got makeup and stuff and better than when I only got it in 8th! She's my mom's pet. Daddy drunk tonight.

December 21, 1968: Today the Apollo 7 went off with three men in it which are going to go to the moon. Important date.

January 7, 1969: A colored lady named Irma is staying with us while Daddy's on trip.

February 17, 1969: I got in a gigantic fight with my mom. She hit me and everything and I cried for 3 hours.

February 18, 1969: Another big fight. She hit me in the car! I hid in the closet. She said that no one likes me. I cried again! I hate her!

May 28, 1969: My mom's going insane.

June 23, 1969: Boring morning but at about 4:00 I went sailing in big boat with Liz and Daddy.

July 8, 1969: Went to beach again. Getting a good tan. Boys were staring at me when went in water.

July 11, 1969: Left on a boat trip with Dad, just the two of us. Was scary tonight because of storm!

July 20, 1969: We've made History! Today U.S.A. landed on the moon! We saw them step on the moon on T.V. Watched long time.

July 21, 1969: The Apollo 11 is coming home now. They docked this morning.

August 4, 1969: Boy did I get in trouble all day! I got hit so, so hard! (by Mom). Was going to tell Dad! I'll be good from now on!

August 12, 1969: Slept with Mark in Tony's bed because Mom's in mine.

August 19, 1969: Larry and Greg came over today and tonight. Fun. Played dating game. I like Larry more and vice versa.

August 21, 1969: Talked to Larry and Greg for an hour on phone while Dad and Mom were gone tonight. Larry said wanted to kiss me. Came over today.

August 22, 1969: Larry and Greg came over but said they were bored and went to beach. Larry called and asked me to join bowling league. Dad said NO!! I don't know why.

September 7, 1969: Went to Arlyn's boy, girl party. Boring until Chris came. He's in 10th. Me and him oldest. We played spin the bottle and another like it. He kissed me all the time. Said I was cute!

September 17, 1969: I found out today that we're going to move. Mom got a phone call from Dad, long distance, and she's upset and crying. Going to Georgia!!

September 18, 1969: Mom got another call. Glad we're going to Alabama instead of Georgia. Moving about 6 weeks to 3 months. Dad and Mom are upset.

September 23, 1969: Finished writing a song I made up (composed). It was 3 pages!

September 24, 1969: In history, there are lots of popular people in my group, the kind that take drugs. Skip (one of them) talks with me and all of them count me in with them.

October 1, 1969: In library a boy came in and sat right across from me. Didn't even see him at first. He started talking to me and asked my name. His name is Charlie. Think he likes me. All he does is stare! (Everywhere on me).

October 5, 1969: Skip talked to me all during Social Studies about drugs. He was told I was moving to Alabama. Says you get life for marijuana. Thinks I take drugs. I hardly understood a thing he said.

October 6, 1969: Saw Charlie again. I wish he would come in library more often cause I haven't talked to him lately. Meanwhile Skip likes me. Another sexpot.

October 7, 1969: In case you didn't know, Charlie is a real bad drug addict. He even takes things like Smack! Charlie asked me out for Friday night. He stares at me all the time. I'm glad he likes me!

October 8, 1969: Sue and I have been planning a way to sneak out to go with Charlie cause I know Dad wouldn't let me. Charlie got kicked out for being stoned today.

October 9, 1969: Talked to Charlie today. He put his arm around me. Told him I couldn't go out and he was really upset. Sue said he asked me my phone number! Good.

October 14, 1969: Wore a new green outfit. It shows off my figure. I look real good in it.

October 15, 1969: Charlie asked me out again but told him I just can't go out. He asked me to take marijuana and asked me if I tried it before. I haven't but I told him someday I will.

October 16, 1969: Charlie got suspended. I don't know what for. He looked good today in his brown jacket. Blair Johnson told me some queer, Jim Kelly, likes me. I hope not.

October 17, 1969: Jim Kelly called me up to ask me to go to the football game. He begged me into going but I didn't go. When he came to pick me up I went to Erin's house.

October 18, 1969: I cried today because I was thinking of how gross I am. If someone like Jim Kelly can like me then I must be pretty gross. I want to be pretty!

October 21, 1969: Been noticing real cute guys staring at me. Makes me feel good.

October 17, 1969: Played football again after school but not with Randy. This time with Mike and Bill. Bill told a guy I had a good BODY! He knew I heard him.

November 1, 1969: Right when I came home from Jones this morning, Mom said, "Pack, we're going to Alabama!" So we've begun our trip and staying in Jacksonville now.

November 2, 1969: Arrived in Alabama today. It sure is beautiful with all the trees and mountains. I love our house, just LOVE it! It's so old-fashioned and cozy. Cute boys down here. Not hillbilly.

November 3, 1969: Spent all day looking at mine and Mark's school. Mine is ugly and is out in the middle of nowhere. Made Mom have anxiety attack.

November 5, 1969: Came home today about 8:30. Mom was crying and everything. Said she didn't want to move. I'm upset. Don't understand how she changes her mind. We aren't moving.

November 9, 1969: We got our pictures Friday and Mom found them. (I hid them. They were terrible). She's already sending them. I'm so ugly. I cried all day and night!!!

November 14, 1969: Mary, Sue, and I played football with some boys. They're really cute. Smoked at Mary's house.

November 16, 1969: Stayed at Mary's all day with Sue. Went to play football but really went down to the main canal on these islands and had a few puffs of cigarettes.

November 27, 1969: Had a very nice Thanksgiving. Watched T.V. all morning, parades and football. Had delicious dinner and wine and dessert. Dad got drunk and sat by the fire.

November 29, 1969: This morning got called home from school. Mom rushed to hospital cause of bleeding ulcer.

December 27, 1969: We went to Bernard Surf to dinner but at 3:00! I had pretty good dinner. After dinner going to car, this hippy I know said hi to me and I was so embarrassed seen with my family.

January 13, 1970: Sue told me that Molly told Skip "Why did you give the cigarette to gross Kathy?" Molly described me as "ugly, weird hair, quiet, and queer." One of these days, I'll commit suicide. (Note: Kathy was the name I went by at school).

January 14, 1970: Skip always talks with me and trying to sell me Acid!

January 25, 1970: My mom has been picking on me. Today I got kicked by Dad because Mom told lies about me to get back at me. I'm tempted to commit suicide with these pills I got.

February 4, 1970: You'll never believe this and I shouldn't write this. But Skip gave me a joint today. I might even try it this weekend the way things have been going with Mom and me.

February 24, 1970: Dad on trip and we just got news that we're moving again back to Virginia. I'm so happy to move back there.

February 17, 1970: Dad came home from his trip tonight. He caught a terrible cold from up north. The news is, we're moving for sure back to Virginia around June.

March 1, 1970: You'll never believe it but I drove the Volkswagen today. Dad took me out to the track at school to learn the clutch and then I drove all over the place! It's fun.

IN THE DIARY I mention getting hit by both Mom and Dad, but I don't mention the times my dad hit Mom. I would hear it from their bedroom. He'd hit her a lot. He'd be drunk and she'd be drugged up.

It's obvious from the diary entries that I despised and hated my mother and a lot of the time despised and hated myself. My mom seemed to have more of a negative influence on me than my dad during this time. I didn't loathe my dad as much as my mom. Dad and I had memorable moments of surfing together, just the two of us going on a boat excursion, and him teaching me how to drive using a clutch. I developed into a pretty girl with a good figure, despite telling myself I was ugly, and enjoyed attention from the boys. However, I seemed to be attracted to the "bad" boys. I was approached by drug users at school and experienced peer pressure, although I didn't do drugs. I loved to play football and fish. I wore braces and played spin-the-bottle. Then I talked of running away and wanting to commit suicide. That was a precursor of what was to come.

«Chapter 15»

WE MOVED FROM COCOA BEACH back to Falls Church, Virginia when I was fifteen years old. We drove in our Volkswagen van, staying at hotels along the way. My sister, two brothers and I sat in the center back seats and my mom was in the very back.

Dad didn't want to make pit stops along the way, so he brought a big pot to use in the car to relieve ourselves. I refused to go to the bathroom in it. My mom was heavily sedated from popping her pills, which she was doing more so those days. She actually peed and pooped in the pot in front of us all and the van reeked with the disgusting odor with the pot unemptied. It was one of the most revolting, mortifying, shameful incidences I've ever experienced.

THE HOUSE WE MOVED INTO was in Lake Barcroft again, right across the street from our old house on the lake. Lake Barcroft was still the upscale neighborhood that we had lived in before. In fact, the first black Supreme Court Justice Thurgood Marshall lived down the street. The prejudice was still there, though. I was told that when the residents of Lake Barcroft heard that Thurgood Marshall was moving into the neighborhood, many of them drew up a petition against him moving in because he was black. They didn't succeed. I had the privilege to meet him. On one occasion, my best friend Michele and I were raising money for a cause and made batches of chocolate chip cookies, selling them door to door. When we knocked on his door he answered and was delighted to buy some from us. He was very friendly. The second time I talked to him, I was doing a paper for my government class and I wanted to get an interview with him for my paper. When I knocked on his door and asked for an interview, he wasn't as friendly and refused. I understand that now. Being in the public eye, he probably didn't want to be quoted.

Our first week in Lake Barcroft, the whole family spent a day at one of the beaches on the lake. I met some other teenagers there and we socialized a bit. They asked me if I wanted to walk in the woods with them which bordered the beach. My parents said it was okay. When we settled in a clearing in the woods, the kids sat around in a circle passing around a joint. I wanted to be accepted by them and be "cool", so I took a few puffs. I didn't like it.

I became friends with a girl who lived across from us in our old house. She was the class president of the high school that I was to attend that fall. She invited me to a party that took place at another kid's house. His parents were away for the weekend. I attended and there was a lot of drinking going on. I had my first drink – Sloe Gin. I drank it straight. It was berry flavored and tasted so good so I drank a lot of it, and then the effects hit me. I became drunk for the first time in my life. I ended up throwing up in the toilet but I experienced what it felt like to lose my inhibitions – I liked it since I was by nature so shy. That was the first of many drinking parties and gatherings I would attend during my junior and senior years.

On one occasion during Halloween, I was out with a group of my best friends and had been drinking too much. We were at McDonald's and they dared me to climb on the roof and yell out, "The Great Pumpkin is coming!" So I did. It was a crack up.

I had long, brown hair to my waist with natural blond highlights and I was tan. I had a good figure and was popular with the boys. I dressed in sexy and provocative outfits which surprisingly my mom allowed. In the summer I wore tank tops and hot pants. Sometimes I dressed like a hippie, though, because I wanted to be "cool", not square. It was the hippie generation where most of us wore bell bottoms, hip huggers, and cotton tops with a flower print. I also wore my favorite suede, floppy hat everywhere I went.

I loved the attention from the boys. It gave me self-esteem. I started dating when I was sixteen years old and experienced my first French kiss and went to "second" and "third" base. I was desperate to feel love and be loved and sex gave me a sense of that. I never had a steady boyfriend and shied away from any kind of real relationship with boys.

But then came along Carlos. I met him in Nags Head, North Carolina where Dad took us for a family vacation. It was another one of his favorite surfing spots. My dad still surfed even though he was in his forties and was still pretty good at it.

I met Carlos on the beach. He was a surfer too. I was sixteen and he was nineteen. He liked me. In fact he told me he loved me at first sight. We were watching my dad surf from the shore and he raved about him. "Your dad is so cool!" he said, which made me feel good.

During our stay there, Carlos and I would make out on the beach at night. He got all friendly with my parents and said he would like to visit us sometime. He lived in Newport News, Virginia. My parents let me give him my phone number and address. I remember during the ride home that I felt like I was in love.

Well sure enough he showed up at our house one day. (I don't remember if Carlos and I had first talked about him coming). He didn't have a car and I think he hitchhiked. My parents let him stay at our house several nights in a row and use our VW bug. He would use it to drive me around, but he'd also take off in it by himself. I'm not sure where he went but my parents didn't seem to care.

One time Carlos took me into Washington D.C. to a Vietnam War protest. I didn't know he was taking me to a protest. We were in the middle of a crowd at the Lincoln Memorial Reflecting Pool near the Washington Monument. Suddenly there was a lot of commotion and I was in the middle of it. The police starting hitting people with their bats, right next to me! Carlos grabbed my hand and we ran and got away. It really scared me.

During his stay at our house, he would sleep with my brothers in their room. One night he came downstairs into my room and said he wanted to make love to me. I said no. I still considered myself a "good girl". Going to third base was one thing. Going all the way was another. He didn't take no for an answer. He said if I loved him I would do it. I didn't want to, but he forced himself on me.

I lost my virginity that night. The next morning I felt dirty, traumatized, numb, and defiled. I felt like a bad girl, especially in God's eyes. I decided that since I committed a great sin and was a bad girl in God's eyes, I didn't have to please Him and be good anymore. I was a sinner and immoral and dirty. I turned my back on God. However, even though I decided I was a sinner and didn't need to be good anymore, I never had intercourse with any other boys the rest of my time in high school.

Carlos continued to come for visits and long stays. Just about every night he would come into my room and have sex with me. I hated it. I never told anyone. I didn't want him to visit anymore. I wanted him gone. By the grace of God, it was a miracle I never got pregnant, having taken no protective measures.

One day after school I called home from a phone booth at school. I was upset. My mom answered. "Mom, either Carlos goes or I go," I said.

She answered harshly, "You tell that to your father."

I was stunned by what she said. I was thinking, "So I'm in trouble for wanting Carlos to leave? Why? She doesn't care?"

Then I figured Mom thought I was being rebellious by stating an ultimatum, and if Dad heard what I said he would think the same and I'd be in trouble. I also figured that I wasn't going to get any support for wanting Carlos to leave. Mom and Dad seemed to love him so much. Given the choice between running away and returning to Carlos still living in our house, I chose to run away. So I did.

It was wintertime and it had been snowing. I didn't know where I was going to go. So my first night I snuck into my best friend's house when no one was home and hid in their closet. I spent the night there. The next morning their dog was sniffing at the closet door. I knew I had to leave. I walked out into the woods and wandered. I decided to spend the next night in the woods, even though it was bitter cold with snow on the ground. I ate the snow to quench my thirst.

In the meantime, my parents called the police. They were looking for me but I didn't know it at the time.

On that cold night in the woods, I decided to go to the house of the Justice of the Peace nearby. I thought, "These will be friendly people and they'll let me stay there."

So I walked to the house and knocked on the door late at night. An old man answered with disheveled hair and an unshaven face. He didn't look friendly.

"Hi. I need a place to stay," I said. "Can I stay for the night?"

He let me in and locked the door. "I'm calling the police," he said.

I cried, "No, please no!"

I tried to escape, but he grabbed my arm and held a firm grip and I couldn't pull myself away. He called the police. Shortly after, the police picked me up and took me to the station. They asked me my name and where I lived. I wouldn't tell them. They asked again and again and I still refused to give them my information. I told them I didn't want to go back home or go back to my parents.

A cop said to me, "Do you want to go to foster care? Because that's where we'll take you."

Then I thought about it. I thought, "No, I don't. I don't want to end up there." So I gave them my information and they called my parents.

Dad picked me up and he looked sympathetic. I wasn't in trouble. On the drive home he said, "I kicked Carlos out. He's gone."

As it turned out, my sister Liz had a talk with Dad while I was gone. She said that she knew Carlos was offering my brothers dope, showing them packets of it. My brothers were only ages thirteen and nine. (Liz didn't know about the other stuff going on between Carlos and me). When Dad heard about the marijuana, he kicked Carlos out. We never saw or heard from him again.

To digress here, I never understood how my parents could welcome a nineteen-year-old man to sleep over at our house days at a time, who was supposedly my boyfriend, when I was only sixteen. It was like he was treated as part of the family. How was this acceptable in my father's eyes? Why wasn't my dad protective of me, like most fathers are of their daughters? Why were both my parents encouraging this relationship?

Because of my mom's mental illness, her behavior was often irrational. Often the way she acted was to be expected.

But my dad's behavior regarding his young teenage daughter? That was and still is a mystery to me.

«Chapter 16»

IN THE LATTER PART OF MY JUNIOR YEAR in high school, I approached my mom and expressed to her that I wanted to see a psychiatrist. I was afraid to tell her though because I felt ashamed about wanting to see one. She had been back to seeing Dr. Morris again, who was the doctor she saw the last time we lived in Falls Church. My mom said she would call Dr. Morris and ask if he would see me. When she did talk to him, he said he would see me on one condition. He said he couldn't have both of us as patients at the same time as a matter of psychiatric principle. Mom decided to stop seeing him so that I could be in therapy with him.

It was very difficult for me to open up and talk to Dr. Morris. What worked best for me was to write down my feelings between our visits, then bring my writings to our sessions for him to read. It was helpful, but he preferred that I talk to him face to face. In time I did.

I continued to see him the rest of my time in high school. I saw him as a father figure, probably just as my mom did. I loved him. I really wanted him to love me. It's that transference thing again. I looked forward to our counseling sessions every week. He did reiterate to me that I saw him as a father figure because my dad wasn't the father I needed and wanted him to be.

I really needed the therapy because I suffered from depression and mood swings and still felt suicidal. One time I took an overdose of Sominex, an over-the-counter sleeping pill. As soon as I took them I called Dr. Morris. (It was really a cry for help). He didn't tell my parents. He said I didn't take enough to kill me. I remember drinking a bunch of caffeinated tea to counteract the effects of the sleeping pills. My parents never found out.

My visits with Dr. Morris were definitely beneficial and helped me cope with the continual struggles I faced while living in a dysfunctional home.

WITH MOM'S ABUSE OF HER medications, I would dread coming home from school not knowing what state she'd be in. "Will she be alert or will she be drugged up?" Then in the evenings I'd be afraid of what state my dad would get in. "Will Dad get drunk tonight and end up in a stupor? Will he be mean tonight?"

I didn't want to bring my friends into my house because my mom embarrassed me. She would be in a catatonic state much of the time. Her behavior disgusted me. For example, she'd be zoned out with her eyes glazed over, in her bathrobe which she stayed in all day, sitting in her Lay-Z-Boy chair eating from a plate in her lap. The only thing is there was nothing on the plate. She'd have a fork and stir it and stir it around the plate and put it in her mouth like she was eating. She would also drool.

Her stomach was always upset and she drank Maalox like it was a glass of milk. The Maalox would leave white paste all around her mouth. She got fatter and fatter. I thought she was a pig. Sometimes I would stand right in front of her and tell her so. She just looked at me with those glazed eyes, oblivious to what I was saying.

Dad was drinking a case of beer on weekends and martinis in the evenings during the work week. It sounds like a cliché, but when he got home he would kick the dog. After his first few drinks, he would get rowdy. He'd continue to play his records louder and louder with the same songs played over and over again. Then as he'd take a few more drinks, he would get in a stupor. One time he was making tacos. He was standing over a hot frying pan with grease preparing to put the tortillas in to brown. We were all at the table waiting for the meal. We were waiting a long time and no food. Then we realized he was just stirring the grease in the frying pan but he wasn't putting the tortillas in. He was just standing over the frying pan doing nothing but stirring.

In the meantime, while I was in eleventh grade, my grades were plummeting. I got C's, D's and F's. I wasn't doing my work and I was skipping school. My parents had me see the school counselor. I liked her and she was helpful. Over time, my grades pulled up and I was able to pass most of my classes. But I couldn't stand the peer pressure and the suffering from shyness at school. Because of this, the first day of school in my senior year, I decided I couldn't cope with going to school anymore. When I came home I told my parents that I just couldn't do it.

They ended up hiring a tutor and she tutored me at home during my senior year. It was just what I needed. I had enough credits to only have to take English Literature and Government. I finished my senior year with A's in both of them. But when it came time for my high school graduation ceremony I didn't want to go. So I didn't even attend my own graduation.

Although I had been shy at school, at home with my neighborhood friends I was outgoing. We had lots of fun but were mischievous. I would sneak out of my window at night. We'd go out drinking, skinny dipping in the lake, exploring "haunted" houses, TP houses, throw raw eggs at cars passing by, and the worst thing we ever did was shoot out street lights with a BB gun. Luckily we didn't get caught. We didn't do drugs but one time I was at a party and a boy introduced me to sniffing glue. I did it a couple of times and my friends were alarmed and worried about me. They told me it would cause brain damage. Fortunately, I stopped doing it. Of course joints and water pipes were passed around at parties. I'd smoke them a few times but I didn't like the effects they had on me at all because of the paranoia I felt. Plus, with Mom being such a prescription drug addict, I didn't like drugs. So I never really got into them.

ALTHOUGH MY MOM AND DAD were dysfunctional parents, they provided my siblings and me special privileges and positive experiences in our childhood that living in affluence enabled. Many families didn't have that. Along with living in upscale neighborhoods, getting a good education, having maids to care for us, experiencing historic moments like the space launches, and taking boating excursions along the Atlantic coast, my parents encouraged and paid for my piano lessons throughout my childhood, which I am forever grateful. They provided a tutor for me in my senior year when I needed it most. At these times they showed they cared. (A therapist once told me later in life, that that might have been my saving grace). Then there were memorable occasions and opportunities like these:

For my eighteenth birthday, my parents took me to the Kennedy Center in D.C., which I celebrated with my closest friends. I dressed up in a fancy gown and enjoyed an expensive dinner with my first legal glass of wine. Another time, my dad took me there for my first concert to hear an orchestra play classical music. It was just him and me. I loved it.

In my senior year, I was privileged to be invited to the debutante ball, which was a very prestigious affair. My parents were so excited for me. Unfortunately, I chose not to go because I thought it was "uncool".

AFTER I GRADUATED FROM HIGH SCHOOL I decided I didn't want to go to college. It seemed everyone expected me to apply to a music conservatory or major in music at a college, as I was a pretty accomplished pianist. But it wasn't the career path I wanted to take. Besides, I was too petrified to play in front of a large audience. It's one thing to play violin in an orchestra and not be the center of attention; it's another thing to be at center stage at a piano. I was afraid to tell my parents that I wasn't ready for college because it had always been so important to them for all of us to go, but they said it wasn't a problem. I knew someday I would go. I just didn't know what my major would be.

I landed my first job as a clerk typist at a government job in Washington, D.C. The company was called "Headquarters U.S. Army Material Command". It wasn't exactly what I had aspired to do, but it brought in the paychecks. My dream was to save up enough money to go to Europe. I wanted to travel. I was still living with my parents at the time but I offered to pay rent, and they accepted.

Then I was finally ready to move out and be on my own. I wanted to move back to Cocoa Beach. Patrick Air Force Base was in a nearby town offering a clerical position, so I applied there and was able to get a transfer from my job in D.C. I was going to live with the parents of a girlfriend of mine across the street from our old house.

So at age eighteen I spread my wings, left the nest, and broke away. Then I entered into the next chapter of my life: adulthood.

PART 2
Adulthood

"For I know the plans I have for you," declares the Lord, "plans to prosper you and not to harm you, plans to give you hope and a future."

(Jeremiah 29:11 NIV)

«Chapter 17»

WHEN I SET OUT ON MY OWN, I didn't know what my future would be. But I knew I wanted freedom from my parents and to live carefree enjoying the beach life in Cocoa Beach. I also knew I didn't want to live there permanently. My ultimate goal was to travel to Europe on my own.

I moved to Cocoa Beach in the spring of 1973 and took up residence with my girlfriend's parents as planned. All I brought with me from home were clothes and a few personal items. I had no car. I started working full-time at Patrick Air Force Base, commuting by bus. Not having many expenses, I put money into savings each payday to use toward my future travels.

It wasn't long before I met a guy who was a marine biologist. We started dating and I ended up moving in with him. I never told my family or friends back home. I didn't love him. I knew I wasn't going to stay with him forever but I never told him that.

We had lots of fun snorkeling at Sebastian Inlet catching Rock Crab, shrimping off a bridge over the Indian River at midnight, clamming at the beach, and fishing off the ocean pier catching large ocean fish like Redfish and Bluefish. We would eat seafood for lunch and dinner, including shrimp and crab salad. It was the good life.

While I was in Cocoa Beach, my family moved to Santa Barbara from Virginia. Mom later told me that Dad got fired for drinking on the job. I never really found out what happened. After thinking it over, I made the decision to move to Santa Barbara as well once I left Florida and after my travels in Europe.

One day at the end of summer I went to a travel agency, reviewed a few guided tours to Europe, and selected one with American Express. I had saved up enough money to go to Europe by then and went ahead and purchased the package. I would be traveling the month of October. I didn't tell my boyfriend about it but he eventually found out. I had written a letter to a girlfriend about my plans and had left the letter on our coffee table before sending it (not very bright of me). He found it and read it. He was in disbelief, realizing that I wasn't planning to return to Cocoa Beach after my travels. Once he confronted me, we talked things over and it turned out he was never committed to a long-term relationship, just as I wasn't. (Obviously, there wasn't much honesty in the relationship). We agreed to part ways.

I was soon on my journey, flying across the Atlantic to my first destination in London. Once I arrived to my hotel room after a long flight, I broke down and cried and thought, "Oh my gosh, what have I done? I'm here all by myself in a foreign country thousands of miles away from home!" It was a scary thought. It didn't help when I went to the bathroom and noticed that there was no toilet paper. Instead, there was a bidet for cleaning your butt, which took me quite a while to figure out how to use! Okay, I really was in a foreign country. But I pulled myself together and prepared myself for the adventure ahead.

I spent a little less than a month in Europe traveling to nine countries: England, Holland, Belgium, Germany, Austria, Switzerland, Liechtenstein, Italy, and France, including the nation of Monaco. Most of the people on my tour were middle-aged and older couples, or honeymooners.

After I got over my initial fear of being in Europe on my own, I felt like I could be anyone I wanted to be, meaning no one knew the "Trink" I had left behind and I wasn't confined to what defined me back home: shyness. I shed my inhibitions. I was sociable and outgoing. Some hotels had pianos and I would entertain the guests. One man on the tour told me, "You could be Miss America."

I found the cultures and people so interesting. For instance, I noticed how proper the British people were. I went to a comedy play in London and when they laughed and clapped, they were so reserved – not boisterous like an American audience can be. The British police wore funny hats – in my eyes. In Italy, drinking was legal at any age, and when I was walking down a cobblestone street I saw a group of young boys, around nine or ten years old, drinking out of a jug of wine. The Italians were very friendly and expressive people and the men seemed to have the "hots" for me. The French weren't so nice. They didn't like

Americans. But their language was so beautiful and so were the women.

I saw so many historic sights all over Europe. It was all so exciting to see Buckingham Palace, the Swiss Alps, the Roman Colosseum, Michelangelo's sculpture of David, the Sistine Chapel, the Leaning Tower of Pisa, the iconic Eiffel Tower, and so much more. Some of my most memorable experiences were being serenaded on a gondola ride in Venice, seeing the Pope wave to us from his balcony at the Vatican and having my grandmother's rosary blessed by him, and visiting the magnificent Notre Dame Cathedral, where I almost fell to my knees overcome by the beauty of the sun shining through the stained glass windows. The whole trip was an unforgettable experience which opened my eyes about the world.

The last leg of the trip was in Paris. I took a flight from Paris to Falls Church for a brief visit with my old friends. Then I flew to Santa Barbara to live with my parents until I could find a job and live on my own. That was a mistake.

«Chapter 18»

IT WAS NOVEMBER 1973 AND I was nineteen years old. I moved in with my parents but there was "no room at the inn," so to speak. I lived in a makeshift room in the garage.

I landed a job as a keypunch operator at Electronic Data Systems (EDS). It was the most boring, depressing job I ever had, entering data from medical records into fields on the computer, all while being timed. They gave out monthly awards for "Keypuncher of the Month" for whoever had the fastest time. I was a recipient of the award myself. Yet it was a mindless job where you had too much time to think.

Mom and Dad hadn't changed. Being back in that environment wasn't good for me. I regressed. In a way, I felt I didn't want to grow up and I wanted to be a child again, trying to squeeze out any ounce of love I could get from my parents. It was like my experiences in Florida and Europe had never happened. I didn't make much of an effort to move out.

I decided to get more serious about piano. I actually considered going to a music conservatory someday, and was seeking a good piano teacher to give me a more solid foundation. I was referred by my aunt to a piano studio in Santa Barbara called "James and Moule", named after the teachers. I auditioned for both instructors and Mr. James accepted me as a student. I ended up taking lessons from him for about two years and it was the best training I ever got. I played pieces from Hayden, Mozart, Beethoven, Chopin, Czerny, Bach, Debussy, Brahms, Schumann, Franz Liszt – all the classical composers. My parents still had the piano from my childhood, so I had a piano to practice on. I would practice endlessly.

One day I was practicing and Dad was home and came up to me irritated and said, "This is driving me crazy! You really think you're going to be accepted into a conservatory? You're dreaming. I don't want to hear it anymore." And he took the piano lid and slammed it down on my hands. That made me so depressed that I snuck into my mother's medicine cabinet and stole her sleeping pills. I decided that I was going to kill myself. I worked the evening shift at work. I took the pills in with me that night and went into the restroom and took a handful of pills. I really didn't want to die and wanted to be found. I didn't realize I took enough pills to kill me.

My supervisor found me in the bathroom unconscious. She called 911 and I was rushed to the hospital. Of course I don't remember any of it. What I do remember is the experience I had before I woke up in the bed at the hospital.

It was partially dark and I was walking on a path, almost like a tunnel, and I was looking straight ahead. I saw willowy figures in the distance and there was a bright light to which I was drawn. It felt loving and accepting and I wanted to go there. I kept walking toward the light and as I got closer, I saw that the figures looked like people with faces I couldn't make out. They came toward me and said, "No, go back, go back!" I felt discouraged because I didn't want to go back.

The next thing I remember was that I was lying down in a bed and I could hear voices but I couldn't see. I shouted out, "I'm a good girl. I'm a good girl."

Then I heard a man's voice reply, "You're not a good girl for doing this."

I started waking up and I realized I was in a hospital room. The man's voice I heard was the doctor.

Later in the day, a nurse came in and said my parents were outside the door and wanted to see me. I said, "I don't want to see my dad." She told them and neither one of them came in to visit.

I was later told that I almost died.

After a brief stay in the hospital, I was admitted to a psychiatric ward. I was required to stay there for at least three days due to rules regarding attempted suicide. The other patients there seemed like crazy people to me. Some would walk around in circles or stand in a corner muttering to themselves. There were schizophrenics and manic depressives. I shared a room with a girl my age and one night she approached my bed and said she wanted to have sex with me. I thought, "I've got to get out of here!"

I knew I wasn't crazy, figuring I was just suffering from depression. I felt shameful though. It felt degrading to be there. I was never given any medication and if they had suggested it I would have refused. I was negatively affected by watching my mom take all those pills and I told myself I would never do that. I didn't even like taking aspirin.

I had sessions with resident psychiatrists but I don't remember our conversations. I think they suggested I look into outpatient therapy after being released.

When I was discharged, I didn't return home. I lived with my grandmother for a short time before finding an apartment of my own. I didn't seek a psychiatrist or psychologist to get therapy. I resumed working at EDS doing data entry on the night shift and continued to take piano lessons. My grandmother had a piano so I was able to practice on hers. During the day I enjoyed going to the beach. It was obviously better for me to not live with my parents. A few months after my suicide attempt, I eventually spoke to my parents again.

MY SISTER AND BROTHER had been going to college. In fact, Liz already had her bachelor's degree and was working on her master's in exercise physiology. Mark was close to getting a bachelor's degree in accounting. Tony was still in high school. I felt envious and in competition with Liz and Mark because here they were earning their college degrees and I felt like I was amounting to nothing. I was beginning to think that pursuing a career in music wasn't for me after all and I also wanted to go to college. I just didn't know what to pursue.

One day a co-worker my age was doing homework during her break and when I looked over her shoulder I asked, "What is that?" She said it was a course in FORTRAN, a computer language. She said she was a computer science major and was attending Santa Barbara City College. I looked at the workbook and said, "That looks interesting. That looks like something I could do."

It planted a seed in my head to major in Computer Science. I was good in math and sciences and was up for the challenge. When I told my uncle about it, who was an electrical engineer working on his Ph.D., he prompted me to go beyond computer science into the field of electrical engineering. I knew that not many women went into the field and I think I wanted to prove to myself that I could do what any man could do – including my father.

I abruptly quit piano lessons and applied for admission to Santa Barbara City College. I had never taken my SATs or ACTs in high school because I was afraid to find out what my scores would be, but they weren't required. The city college was inexpensive enough for me to afford it on my own as long as I was working. My parents didn't offer. So I started enrolling in classes. I found my life more stable while in school. It made me feel more sane and self-confident. It made me feel normal. It was a turning point in my life.

In the meantime, my parents had bought a five-acre ranch in Santa Ynez, just over the foothills from Santa

Barbara, and Tony attended high school there. On the ranch, they boarded horses and had cows, chickens, rabbits, ducks in the backyard pond, turkeys, and even a goat. I would visit often. The goat became my pet and I named him "Ronnie" after Ronald Reagan who was president at the time. Ronald Reagan had a ranch in Santa Ynez and often during his retreats from The White House we'd see his military helicopter flying over us from the airport in Santa Barbara to his ranch. Ronnie became a nuisance though as goats often do. He was being destructive to the flower beds, the fence, and areas around the house. But we all still loved him … or so it seemed.

One day I was over at the house for dinner with Mom and Dad. It was a basic meal of meat, potatoes and vegetables. After we finished, my parents asked me, "How did you like the meat?"

"It tasted different," I said.

They said to me, "That was Ronnie." Both my mom and dad roared with laughter. They thought it was so funny. I was horrified and ran to the bathroom, sick to my stomach.

«Chapter 19»

I WAS AT MY PARENT'S HOME in Santa Ynez and Mom was in her Lay-Z-Boy chair in her bathrobe, drooling, eyes glazed over and about to pop another pill. I cried out, "Mom, don't."

Dad heard me and stood over me and shouted, "If you ever say that again I'll beat your head in! She needs her pills." He scared me so much I almost peed in my pants. Later I figured out that my dad was an "enabler" and liked dominating her and having her under his thumb.

Mom wasn't seeing a psychiatrist at the time but she had a primary care physician who was maintaining her medications. I decided to make an appointment with him to tell him about Mom. I told him what a zombie Mom was and that she would take pills all day long. I said she could barely function. He really took me seriously. He said he would address it by slowly weaning her off her medications.

I was at my mom and dad's house one day when Mom got a call from the doctor. I heard her end of the conversation and she started flipping out. "You can't do this! I need these medications!"

The doctor did start weening her off (although he kept her on a drug called Mellaril which was used to treat psychotic disorders) and as Mom was coming off the medications, she acted like a wild animal breaking out of a cage, roaring like a lion with boldness and fierceness. She wasn't a drugged up zombie sitting in her Lay-Z-Boy chair in her bathrobe all day, eating from a plate with no food on it and drooling with Maalox pasted all around her lips and mouth. She got dressed in the morning all raring to go and gave everyone hell. She even lost a bunch of weight. Dad didn't know what to think. I never told anyone that I had spoken to her doctor.

Months later during Christmas, Dad told my siblings and me he had something important to tell us. Mom must have been in the bedroom asleep, but the rest of us were all gathered in the family room when Dad made the pronouncement: "I'm getting a divorce."

I remember the expression on Mark's face. It was stricken with shock. I'm thinking, "Yay! The truth is out. It's about time. This is better for all of us!"

After twenty-five years of marriage, Mom and Dad got a divorce. They sold the house and Dad bought a small house in a neighboring town. Mom moved to Isla Vista near Santa Barbara and rented an apartment. From that time on, Mom was a changed person – for the better.

Mom was driving again. More surprisingly than that, she got a job as a secretary at a radio station in Santa Barbara. She was seeing a psychiatrist at the time and he must have been good because I never saw anyone make such a 180-degree turn for the better in all my life.

«Chapter 20»

I WAS CONTINUING MY EDUCATION at the city college, working part-time at EDS and making a little extra money tutoring in physics, algebra, and calculus along with being a teacher's assistant for an introductory physics class. I attended the city college for three years before getting a transfer to UCSB as an electrical and computer engineering major. I earned a 3.97 GPA at Santa Barbara City College and received scholarships to help pay for my tuition at UCSB. I was one of the very few female electrical engineering students in my class.

I remember one male student telling me, "This major is hard. You'll end up dropping out." That made me even more determined. Again I thought, "I can do what any man can do. I'm as smart as they are."

Interesting that my dad was an aerospace engineer and I was going into the same field.

During the time I was in college, I met Scott. He had been working for my uncle at a golf shop and was introduced to me by my aunt. I liked him. He was red-headed with freckles and not the surfer type I was usually attracted to, but he was real friendly and funny—a nice guy. We started dating and got more serious about each other. He was an excellent golfer and aspired to be a professional golfer on the PGA tour. I was attracted to him not just because of his outgoing personality, but because he seemed to come from a very wholesome family, the kind of family I didn't have. His family also lived in Santa Ynez near my parents. I spent a lot of time with his family.

Scott and I eventually moved in together. I was finishing up my junior and senior years at UCSB. The summer after my junior year, my brother, Mark, and I backpacked around northern Europe visiting England, Holland, Germany, Denmark, Norway and Sweden. It was another experience of a lifetime. I knew that this was the time to get in all my traveling because once I graduated from college, landed a professional job, got married and had kids, there wouldn't be another opportunity for a long time.

I graduated from UCSB with a degree in Electrical and Computer Engineering in May of 1983, putting myself through 100%. There were less than 1% women in my graduating class. In July I landed a job as a software engineer with Santa Barbara Research Center. In August Scott and I married and soon after, Scott turned pro and started traveling on the golf circuit around southern California, Florida, and Arizona. Life was good. My life had finally turned around. And I looked forward to having children.

Soon after Scott and I married, I got pregnant. I was so happy. As soon as I found out, I told all my friends and family, even my boss at work. Unfortunately, I miscarried when I was about nine weeks along. I not only grieved over the loss but I was worried that I could never have children. It was what I wanted most in my life – to have children. But only months later, I got pregnant again and my daughter was born in November 1984 when I was thirty years old. I was SO happy.

I would have liked to have been a stay-at-home mom and have more babies but Scott wasn't making the cut in the golf circuit and not bringing in enough money. I solely supported the family and helped fund his tours.

I had to return to work ten weeks after my daughter was born and put her in daycare. I had paid an agency to refer me to daycare providers, but after trying each of them out for a week or so, I found the quality of their care unacceptable. I hired and fired several of them before leaving my daughter with a cousin who cared for five other infants. I felt like I had traumatized my daughter, and it traumatized me. As I dropped my baby off at daycare, I choked back sobs. I felt my daughter needed to be home with her mommy. What didn't help is that once I did return to work, I got my first annual review. I was sitting before my boss in his office expecting feedback and ratings on my past year's performance. Instead he said to me point blank, "You should be home being a mom, not here working. It's not good for the child." He gave me a poor review, not based on my performance, but based on his opinion that I shouldn't be a working mom.

My mom got laid off from the radio station when it was bought by another company. For a while she babysat two little boys whose mother was a mail carrier. I thought it over and I felt the best caregiver for my daughter was my mother. I pleaded to her to be my daycare provider, with pay. She agreed and began watching my baby girl. When I gave birth to two more daughters, two years apart, she cared for them as well while I worked.

My mother became the girls' second mom. She was not only a wonderful grandmother but she cared for my children in the way that I had always yearned for when I was a child. She was a blessing to me and the girls. She took the girls to their piano, ballet, and tap dance lessons, to the beach and the park, outings to the donut shop and local diner, and drove them to and from school as they got older. She was energetic and affectionate. She was a lifesaver.

I loved being a mom. My girls meant everything to me and made me so happy. I was determined not to be the mom my mother was to me when I grew up. I had a full-time job, but outside of work I spent every minute with my girls. I loved them so much and tried to provide them the best childhood possible, the one I didn't get.

In the meantime, Scott's golfing career took off and he continued to travel a lot and started bringing home some income. However, our marriage was not doing well. I knew that as a golfing professional he would be traveling a lot, but even when he was home from the circuit he rarely spent time with me and the girls. He never grew up. He'd be out with the boys playing poker, playing in baseball and basketball leagues, and playing recreational golf with his friends. He missed parent/teacher conferences, school performances, recitals, birthday parties, and other family gatherings. He was also very irresponsible with our finances, which I would try to manage, and I continued to nag him about his overspending.

During this time, my oldest daughter had to have five eye surgeries for severely crossed eyes, which were performed at UCLA Medical Center. Her surgeries were from age ten months to five years old. Scott wasn't there for some of the surgeries since he was on the tour. That was hard on me. I basically felt like a single parent and didn't have his emotional support.

One day I read a book by Dan Kiley called, "The Peter Pan Syndrome – Men who have never grown up". The author described the Peter Pan Syndrome as an adult who doesn't want to take responsibilities and mature. I thought, "That's my husband." More interestingly, the author said the wife of a "Peter Pan" husband was enabling him by picking up the slack. Quoting a licensed psychotherapist, Marni Feuerman:

"You must stop your own enabling and dysfunctional behavior to get out of this challenging dynamic. You have to realize that you are part of the reason that your spouse continues to act the way he does. Think back to your childhood. Were you made to grow up too fast or be overly responsible? Maybe you had to take care of an alcoholic or neglectful parent. Were you

in charge of your younger siblings? You most likely got stuck in such a role, then brought your care-taking behavior into adulthood, including your current romantic relationships."

"Wow," I thought, "That's me."

One day, after seven years of marriage, Scott came home from one of his trips and told me he was leaving me. He moved out. A few weeks later I found out I was pregnant with our fourth child.

Here I was pregnant, separated from my husband with three kids, ages five, three, and one. I called a Christian couple who attended a church I had recently attended, which wasn't Catholic. They told me to open my bible to James (NASB). As I read these verses, the pages glowed. There was light and I understood. These were the words that impacted me the most:

"Consider it all joy, my brethren, when you encounter various trials, knowing that the testing of your faith produces endurance." (James 1:2-3)

"But he must ask in faith without any doubting, for the one who doubts is like the surf of the sea, driven and tossed by the wind." (James 1:6)

"Blessed is a man who perseveres under trial; for once he has been approved, he will receive the crown of life which the Lord has

promised to those who love Him. (James 1:12)

"Every good thing given and every perfect gift is from above, coming down from the Father of lights, with whom there is no variation or shifting shadow." (James 1:17)

I realized I had a loving Father on whom I could depend – with whom there is no variation or shifting shadow, unlike my dad. God is the Father of lights, not darkness. He was the only one I could depend on at that moment. He understood my trials and had compassion. I no longer felt ashamed and dirty. I felt loved for who I was, even with all my messiness. God no longer felt distant, stern and cold, who hid His face from me and was only there to judge. Instead I felt loved, accepted, and purified. I felt the Holy Spirit within me, the warmth inside.

I was saved.

Scott and I attempted marriage counseling for a few weeks and I tried to tell Scott about my salvation, how it had changed me, and hoped that he would see the light too, but to no avail. We were divorced soon after. I also miscarried.

Mom was there for me. She continued to watch the girls while I worked full-time. I don't know what I would have done without her.

REGARDING MY FATHER, a few years after Mom and Dad divorced, Dad remarried and lived in Santa Maria with his new wife. He worked at Vandenberg Air Force Base on the space shuttle program. Then on January 28, 1986, the space shuttle Challenger exploded just after blasting off from Florida's Kennedy Space Center, killing all seven astronauts on board, including a civilian teacher. The disaster brought the U.S. civilian space program to an abrupt halt. Because of this, Dad was forced to take early retirement.

Dad's drinking didn't stop. He would drink day and night, starting the morning off with a screwdriver cocktail. He became a sloppy drunk and I could tell that his drinking definitely killed a few brain cells. I avoided seeing him or talking to him. I didn't feel bitter. I just realized that it was not only unhealthy for me to be around him anymore, but also bad for my children to see him drunk. Our communication became scarce.

AFTER MY SALVATION, I was on fire for the Lord and wanted to find ways to serve Him. God opened a door.

When my maternal grandmother died, I played the piano at her funeral. Since I was so shy, I had hardly played the piano for anyone but for myself. But my family asked me to play at the service, so I did.

An elderly couple from my church attended the funeral. Afterward, they came up to me and said, "You've attended our church all this time and you've never shared your talent? You must play for us. We'll have our music director listen to you."

I played for the music director of the church a few days later, reluctantly, since I thought I could never play in front of a large group of people. Being raised a Catholic I didn't know any hymns or Christian songs so I played classical music and some contemporary. He said, "God has given you a talent to share, not to hide in your living room. This is how you can serve Him."

He was right. God gave me a talent and I needed to use it for His glory. The organist and excellent pianist gave me a book of hymns and gospel songs, most of which I had never heard before, and I fell in love with them. I played the offertory the following week with all my heart but with much stage fright. But I did it, touching many hearts. I continued to play offertories, accompany the choir, and play on the worship team for years to come.

«Chapter 21»

After my divorce, I grieved, not only for myself but for my children, because they were now living in a broken home having divorced parents. My All-American dream of raising a "Leave it to Beaver" family was shattered.

Here I was, single-parenting a five-year-old entering kindergarten, a three-year-old toddler, and a one-year-old still in diapers while working full-time. It was exhausting. But I did my best to give them a happy childhood. Singlehandedly, I threw large birthday parties with a piñata, with about fifteen to twenty girls. I hosted slumber parties. I took my daughters to the circus and carnivals when they were in town. I brought them to the beach on weekends or to the pool at our condo complex. I transported them to their ballet and tap dance lessons on Saturdays and attended their performances and piano recitals.

On Sunday mornings, I managed to get them all dressed in pretty dresses and French-braided their hair for church. Then at church while they were in Sunday school, I played the piano and keyboard during the service. I practiced the piano on weeknights after the girls were tucked into bed. They tell me to this day that they have fond memories of listening to me play, serenading them to sleep.

After I came home from work, I fed them, did homework with them, bathed them, read to them, said prayers with them at night, and tucked them in. I was beat by then end of the day.

I tried to make the holidays a special time for them, especially Christmas. Usually, it was just my Mom celebrating with us. I strived to be cheery around them and make these times festive.

For a while, I cut my work hours back to thirty-six hours a week to have Monday mornings off. That enabled me to volunteer in the kindergarten classroom when my oldest attended, then later when my middle child attended. I also volunteered at the nursery school as the secretary on the board. I did all this while holding down a demanding job as a professional software engineer.

Then there were the times when they were sick – including when all of them came down with the chicken pox. One night my five-year-old woke up in the middle of the night struggling to breath. She had croup. I ran a hot shower and had her breathe in the steam, but it didn't work. I ended up taking her to the ER about two in the morning. But since I was a single parent and didn't have anyone to stay with my three-year-old and one-year-old, I had to wake them up and load all three of them into the car. So here were all three of my young children in an emergency room in the wee hours of the morning. Incidents like this happened more than once.

One time my middle child, then four years old, woke up about 5:30 am with a severe headache, throwing up, and complaining of a stiff neck.

Somehow I suspected spinal meningitis. I called the doctor and he said to come to the office as soon as it opened. I called my mom to stay with the other girls. Once my daughter was examined by the doctor, he also suspected spinal meningitis and told me to drive her immediately to the hospital and he would meet me there. After we got there, he did a spinal tap on her. I wasn't allowed in the room. I could hear her screaming for her mommy down the hallway. It immediately triggered my experience as a child in the hospital with a broken leg when my mommy wasn't with me. It tore me apart.

She was admitted to a hospital room and was very listless and stayed asleep for the next few days. We had to wait three days for the results of the spinal tap. It was agonizing waiting those three days while my little girl remained in a listless state. Her dad didn't show up for a couple of days because he was on a golf tour. I slept every night with her for the next six days.

The results finally came back and she was diagnosed with viral spinal meningitis, which, thankfully, isn't as serious as bacterial meningitis. She bounced back by the end of the week with no harm done to her physically. (As it turned out, hers was the first reported case in history of spinal meningitis in Santa Barbara County and it started an outbreak in the region. She was attending preschool at the time and the other parents were pretty concerned that their own children were exposed. It turned out no one at the school caught it. However, throughout Santa Barbara, some adults and children, even a baby, came down with it. No one ever had an explanation of how my daughter contracted it).

Also difficult for me the first few months after the divorce was the girls' visitation times with their father. I remember the first weekend visitation when he picked them up from our condo, and the girls and I waved goodbye to each other as they pulled away. I cried and cried, sitting in my empty house. It was also hard to alternate having them for the holidays each year between my ex-husband and me. I spent some Christmas, Thanksgiving, and Easter holidays without my children. That's the life of a divorced parent.

Needless to say, single-parenting was hard, especially with three little ones. I tried to be supermom. I wanted the best for them. I think I did a pretty good job considering all the obstacles I had to face.

«Chapter 22»

FOR THE NEXT FOUR YEARS after my divorce, I didn't date. I had Jesus. He came first, and after Jesus came my children.

One day at work, we were told that our department was being moved to Los Angeles. Unless I moved to L.A., I would lose my job. I panicked. I couldn't move to L.A. with the crime, congestion, pollution, knowing no one, and away from my mother and family. I frantically looked for work in Santa Barbara. What was I going to do? How was I going to support the family? I received child support but that wasn't enough to cover all expenses.

Ted was a man with whom I worked in the same department. He became a handyman around the house. Being a single parent, I needed help now and then. Ted showed a likeness toward me. He wasn't a Christian so I wanted only to be friends, believing that if I ever married again, my husband would have to be a Christian. However, one day a friend of mine witnessed to Ted, professing Christ, and told me that Ted had accepted Jesus – just like that, in one day. I believed it was for real and when Ted asked me out for a date, I accepted. I fell head over heels in love with him. It all happened so fast. In only months we were engaged and soon afterward we were married in July, 1994.

In retrospect, I think I was so concerned about losing my job that when a man came along, who I thought was sent by God to save me, I fell for him.

Our marriage had problems from the start. Ted turned out to be authoritative and abusive. He was also influenced by a strange member of our church who was anti-government and a survivalist and who was later banned from attending. Ted started reading all this weird, corruptive material, becoming a survivalist himself, and the first signs of his changed behavior were that he didn't believe in filing our taxes, registering the car, or getting a driver's license. I pleaded to the elders and the pastor of our church to help. They did try to talk to him but it only made Ted angrier. I didn't believe in divorce except for the reasons the bible gives, as when the unbeliever leaves or infidelity, so I wasn't going to divorce him. I tried to make it work but it was hell. (Note: To this day I haven't been able to come to terms with the biblical belief that spousal abuse is not an acceptable reason to divorce).

Before our department closed, Ted found a job in Boulder, Colorado with an aerospace firm. Ted had a daughter and son-in-law living in Louisville and he thought this was ideal. Neither of us could find other work in Santa Barbara so Colorado sounded appealing. We decided to move. We moved on my birthday in September, 1995.

It was a very scary time for me. I lost my job of thirteen years and didn't have a new one to go to; I left my home of twenty-two years; I left my church family; I left my mom; and the girls left their dad and grandmother. I had no friends or family in Colorado. I also couldn't sell my condo, couldn't get enough rent to cover the mortgage payments, and couldn't afford the difference. I had to foreclose and declare bankruptcy to protect my 401K.

About six weeks after we moved to Lafayette, I found a part-time job as a contractor in software engineering. I felt a little more secure. We also found a nice church in Boulder. Soon the girls' father, Scott, moved to Lafayette from California to be near them, which was good for all of them. He eventually remarried and had another daughter.

THIS IS A GOOD TIME to explain my name, "Trink" or "Trinkie". My formal name is Katherine Theresa. The story goes that when I was born, my mother was ill and needed help caring for me. My parents hired a Swedish nursemaid. She called me "Katrinka". My parents liked that name and started calling me Katrinka.

When my sister was a toddler, she couldn't pronounce the name Katrinka and shortened it to "Trinka". So that stuck for a while. When my brother, three years younger than me, started talking, he called me "Trinkie". From that point on my family and friends, including aunts, uncles, cousins, and grandmas, called me Trink or Trinkie. At school, I went by Katherine or Kathy (which I never liked). But even in my professional job in Santa Barbara, I went by Trink.

When we moved to Colorado, I felt it was time to change my name to a less childish name. I chose "Katie" which later got shortened to "Kate". But to this day, my family and childhood friends call me Trink.

«Chapter 23»

WHEN TED AND I PURCHASED our first house in Lafayette (although my name wasn't on the title), he obtained his own P.O. Box, not wanting the government or any other public agency knowing where he lived. In the basement, he had the concrete floor drilled to put a large safe in which he stored silver that he purchased for cash. He didn't trust putting his money in the bank, fearing economic collapse and the government seizing bank accounts. He strongly believed in the militia with the belief that the rise of a tyrannical government in the U.S. was imminent and that it must be confronted through armed force. I don't know if Ted also had weapons and ammunition stashed away in his safe.

One day I had spent the whole day cleaning the house, which was a large two-story home. When he came home from work and I told him proudly that the house was all nice and clean, he ran his finger along the window sills, dust dirtied his fingers, and he exclaimed, "You call this a clean house!"

Then he looked at the carpet and said I did a lousy job vacuuming. He had his own vacuum which was one of those fancy Kirby vacuums with a water tank, and he vacuumed the whole house all over again. "If you want it done right, use this vacuum. Yours is a piece of junk," he barked.

For dinner, I made spaghetti and he complained that I had broken the spaghetti noodles in half and that no real Italian would dare break the spaghetti noodles. He told me his ex-wife was a better cook than I was.

Another time, we were driving back from church on a cold wintery day and for the first time I saw the beautiful hoarfrost that you often see in Colorado, with its white ice crystals glistening on the trees. I exclaimed, "Ted, isn't it beautiful? Look at the trees!"

He didn't answer.

I said again, "Isn't it beautiful?"

He didn't answer.

I asked, "Ted, did you hear me?"

He snapped back, "Of course I heard you. Do you think I'm blind and deaf?"

Other times Ted would get out the bible and repeat the verse:

"Wives, submit yourselves to your own husbands as you do to the Lord. For the husband is the head of the wife as Christ is the head of the church, his body, of which he is the Savior. Now as the church submits to Christ, so also wives should submit to their husbands in everything." (Ephesians 5:22-34 NIV)

"You shall submit to me," he said.

These are just a few examples of the emotional abuse I endured daily. But there was also some physical abuse. After an argument in our bedroom I got so upset I told him I was going to commit suicide. He grabbed me and twisted my arm back, pulled me to the floor, sat on top of me, put his hands around my neck, and proceeded to strangle me. I was gagging and thought I was going to die. He eventually released his grip. I ran out of the bedroom and thought about calling the police, but I was afraid and called the pastor from our church instead. I was crying hysterically telling him what happened. He said he would be over right away to talk to us.

He and his wife showed up at our house quickly. Ted was willing to talk to them. I was still crying uncontrollably and said he tried to strangle me. Ted told the pastor and his wife that I was threatening to commit suicide and that he performed a maneuver that he had learned in the army that you use on your opponent. The pastor only responded, "If you two continue going on like this, you're going to end up in a divorce!" He turned to me and told me to get myself together.

That wasn't the last time Ted tried to strangle me. But the daily emotional abuse to me and the children was much worse than the physical abuse.

I was at the lowest point in my life. I felt so trapped and hopeless. I had nowhere to go. There seemed to be no way out. I felt more and more suicidal but mostly it was a cry for help.

The next time I told Ted I wanted to commit suicide he informed the police. I knew that if the police came, they would take me to the psychiatric ward, so I ran away. I ran into the woods nearby and hid. The police did arrive at the house and started looking for me. I saw them coming in my direction and started running. I ran out into a clearing behind a supermarket. The police caught me, tackled me to the ground as I was struggling, and handcuffed me. There were onlookers in the parking lot. It was humiliating and embarrassing. The police took me in their police car to the psych ward as I had feared. I was required to stay there for at least three days. I felt like I was going insane. And I didn't feel I was understood or treated well by the staff. It seemed they were convinced that I *was* insane.

The doctors wanted to put me on antidepressants but because of what my mother went through, I didn't want to touch them. I was eventually introduced to an outpatient psychiatrist whose main function was not psychotherapy, but prescribing medications deemed necessary to treat certain psychological disorders. I saw him on a weekly basis and he originally diagnosed me with depression, putting me on antidepressants. However, after visiting him for a few months, he finally diagnosed me as having bipolar II disorder.

Bipolar disorder is a mental health condition defined by periods (better known as episodes) of extreme mood disturbances, affecting a person's mood, thoughts, and behavior. There are two main types of bipolar disorders: bipolar I and bipolar II. Bipolar I disorder involves episodes of severe mania and often depression, otherwise known as Manic Depression.

Manic states often involve feelings of euphoria. Bipolar II disorder involves a less severe form of mania called hypomania, along with severe major depressive episodes. My doctor used to call my hypomania episodes "dysphoria" in which I felt not euphoria but irritability, anxiousness, and hyperactivity. My doctor told me I had a brain chemical imbalance, especially with my parents' history. He explained in laymen terms that it's like the nerve cells in my brain "misfire", caused by too much or too little of certain chemicals called neurotransmitters.

He wanted to try out some medications on me but I was very hesitant and I couldn't convince myself that I was bipolar in the first place. I thought the reason for my suicidal feelings was because of my circumstances, not because of some brain chemical imbalance. I also didn't want to take drugs like my mother did. But the doctor said these drugs weren't mind altering. He said having a bipolar disorder is like having epilepsy or diabetes – they are physiological disorders and have to be treated by medication that helps the brain to function correctly. He said I probably had the bipolar disorder back when I was a teenager. I agreed to try out the medications. It took a while to find the right ones that were effective.

Even with the medications, I was in and out of the psychiatric ward a few times, usually admitting myself, with only about a three-day stay each time. At this time, I had a decent, full-time job at Raytheon Corporation in Boulder as a software engineer and didn't want to lose it. I would try to time my stays at the hospital to occur over the weekends so as not to miss work, and when the girls were on visitation with their dad so I could hide it from them.

In conjunction with seeing the psychiatrist, I saw a psychologist for therapy but I can't say he was of much help. I knew my real problem was Ted and the psychologist made me feel 'I' was the problem because of my bipolar disorder. I was a victim of abuse. I wasn't the only one. My children weren't spared.

There was an incident of abuse that involved my nine-year-old daughter where I had to take her to the ER in the middle of the night and she required stitches on her face. I actually called her father to meet me at the hospital, but not telling him what really happened. I cried in his arms. In desperation, I said to the ER doctor, "Please do your best to not leave a scar when you stitch her up."

When I got back from the ER, I called the police. One lady officer sat with me and listened, while the other officer was in the other room with Ted. I could hear him telling her that I was crazy and making the whole thing up. The lady officer I was speaking to believed me. I told her I wanted to press charges. So I did.

I moved out of the house with the girls and stayed temporarily with friends from church. When I went to the district attorney's office to sign the papers for the charges made, I chickened out.

I thought, "Where am I to go? My mother lives in a one-bedroom apartment in Santa Barbara. I can't move in with her. My dad would never take me and the girls in and I wouldn't want to live with him anyway. I have nowhere to go."

When I told the district attorney I wanted to drop the charges he asked with concern, "Are you sure you want to do this? Are you sure?"

"Yes," I said.

The girls and I moved back home and Ted moved down into the basement. That's how we continued to live.

A few families from church took the girls and me in at different times when I needed a separation. Elders tried to talk to Ted. They tried to help, but no one really knew what happened behind our closed doors and Ted had most people at the church believing that I was mentally ill. He was on his best behavior in public. Maybe I had a nervous breakdown, but it's hard to understand what emotional abuse does to a person when you haven't gone through it yourself.

"Emotional abuse is one of the hardest forms of abuse to recognize. It can be subtle and insidious or overt and manipulative. Either way, it chips away at the victim's self-esteem and they begin to doubt their perceptions and reality.

The underlying goal in emotional abuse is to control the victim by discrediting, isolating, and silencing.
In the end, the victim feels trapped. They are often too wounded to endure the relationship any longer, but also too afraid to leave. So the cycle just repeats itself until something is done." – Sherri Gordon

This was the lowest point in my life. God seemed so distant and there was no hope. When I first became a Christian and was so on fire for the Lord, I thought that I would never let God down and that I would never be distant from Him. I would not have dreamed that I would face the circumstances I was going through – how could God allow it? I felt shamed, disgraced, and like a failure – as a mother and to God – although I still tried to be the best mom I could be and loved and adored the girls. I tried to protect them and didn't want anything to happen to them.

One day I was at work and my twelve-year-old daughter called. She asked, "What's going on with Ted? He's got his pickup truck and a U-Haul parked on the street and he's packing them with boxes and furniture."

"What?!" I exclaimed.

I rushed home to find him about to pull away from the house. "Where are you going?" I asked.

He said, "I'm leaving. I'm going back to Santa Barbara."

That was the best thing that could ever happen.

Soon after, I filed for divorce. Thankfully, at that time I had a full-time job with medical benefits to support the family.

Holding true to the bible, I felt justified:

"Yet if the unbelieving one leaves, let him leave; the brother or the sister is not under bondage in such cases, but God has called us to peace." (1 Corinthians 7:15 NASB)

However, I'm going to state again that I still don't understand why the bible states that abandonment and infidelity of a spouse are the only acceptable reasons for divorce. One of the reasons I stayed with Ted was because the church was telling me it was a sin to divorce. But it almost killed me and it was hell. I truly believed that Ted was demon possessed.

I did see Ted again after I filed for divorce since we both had to attend divorce hearings at the courthouse in Colorado. It was an agonizing process, both outside and inside the courtroom, where I felt slandered, attacked, angry, fearful, anxious, exhausted, and traumatized. It took about a year for the divorce to be finalized – in the fall of 1998. After that, I never saw him again.

«Chapter 24»

AFTER TED LEFT ME, I LEFT the church we had been attending and tried out another one. Many of my relationships in the church had been damaged during my marriage to Ted and I didn't feel welcomed or comfortable going there anymore.

I was a single parent of three elementary school children and didn't quite fit in with the culture of the new church I started attending. There weren't many single parents who attended there and since I was divorced, I felt disapproval from many of the members. I didn't have much of a support system although I did make a few friends, mostly couples, who made me feel accepted. Because of a limited support system and social life, I was ready to look elsewhere.

One day I was told by a friend about a wonderful Christian singles group associated with another church in the area. He told me about a singles function coming up which was a woman's birthday party, so I was brave and attended. I wasn't seeking a relationship with a man. I just wanted to make friends with other single people my age. When I arrived at the party, I didn't know a soul except the friend who had accompanied me. I was extremely shy but socialized as best as I could. I found out that most people there were my age and were single parents. That was a good start.

As the party was coming to an end, a jovial man with a big smile on his face approached me and introduced himself. He had a tiny braid on the back of his head, even though he was bald on top. He was wearing a black leather jacket, had a beard and rosy cheeks, and looked and acted like a genuine Santa Claus with the round belly to boot. He just chattered away with me with a jolly laugh and was so friendly. He made me feel at ease. I thought he was a really nice guy. His name was Mike.

Mike told me he was having a Toga party at his house the following day as part of the singles group. He invited me to come. He wasn't asking me on a date. He was just welcoming me to attend the party. I told him I would go.

The funny thing is, I had never heard of a Toga party. I later asked a friend and she said, "You just need to show up in a Toga."

"And where do I get a Toga?" I asked.

She answered, "You just need a sheet and a brooch."

I had a sheet. She had the brooch. And so the next day I went to the party in my sheet held together with the brooch, wearing my bathing suit underneath.

Mike served all finger foods at his party, such as large turkey legs, corn on the cob with melted butter, artichoke, Cornish hens, grapes, dates, nuts and fruit. There must have been fifty people there and I recognized many of the same faces from the party the day before. There was line dancing in his living room, a game of darts, and a Jacuzzi to use in his backyard. I was a wallflower until Mike started to play darts with me. We were on one team and another couple was on the other. Playing darts got me out of my shell a little bit since I love to play games and enjoy competition. Again, Mike made me feel at ease. He was so busy though, running around conducting the party like a chicken with his head cut off.

As the party was winding down and I was leaving, he walked me to the door. "Would you like to stay the night?" He asked. "It's dark and you have a long drive home." I'm thinking, "Man, he's pretty forward. What is he thinking?" So I declined.

He asked a friend for my phone number and called me a few days later. We chatted on the phone a while and I was telling him that I was from California and missed visiting my mother. He said, "Wow. I'm from California too and also have family there. If you ever want to visit your mother, I'd gladly drive you there." Again I'm thinking, "He's really forward!" I declined again. But he asked me out for a date and I accepted.

As I got to know Mike more, I discovered that he had no ulterior motives in asking me to stay at his house the night of his Toga party or when offering to drive me to California. He was genuinely a nice guy and had no intentions of taking advantage of me. He was just that kind of man.

On one of our dates, after I had a couple of drinks and was less inhibited, I told him that I didn't like his ponytail. I didn't say it in a mean way. Just in a matter-of-fact sort of way. He didn't seem to take offense.

On our next date he showed up at my front door with a big smile on his face. He said, "Well?"

I said, "Well what?"

He turned around and I noticed his ponytail was gone. I actually felt bad because I thought, "He really likes me and did this for me and I'm not committed to him yet. What if this doesn't work out? He wouldn't have his ponytail anymore." But I was so flattered.

He really did fall head over heels for me but I kept him at bay. After being through two divorces, and especially after the horrific marriage with my second husband, not surprisingly, I had trust issues. He had been divorced himself, with two adult children of his own, but it had been several years and he was ready for a serious relationship. He told me, "I'm not dating you just to date you. I'm not looking for a 'hood ornament'. I'm looking for a wife."

I had even told him that I had bipolar disorder and he said, "No problem. I see you as a real lady having a gentle spirit, a loving soul, and a good heart. You're a strong Christian, gorgeous, very smart, and VERY sexy. And you're a good mom and should be proud of how you raised the girls."

He didn't judge me. I thought he would think less of me when I told him I was bipolar. He didn't. He accepted me for who I was and saw through my exterior. He saw through to my core. He brought out the best in me and saw the best in me. I felt more stable around him. He evened me out. We were opposites in personality but had so many of the same interests and beliefs. We were so compatible. He made me laugh. I was so happy around him. He made me feel so loved, a love I had never experienced before.

But I was afraid of commitment and I did something that I would always regret. We had planned for him to come to my house and make dinner and he would bring over the groceries. I was so nervous about it that when he came to the door with a bag of groceries in each hand, all smiles, I told him something had come up and that I couldn't have dinner with him. He looked at me with a stunned expression on his face and just said "okay" and walked away. He later called me and said he was breaking up with me. After he said that, I just started crying. I cried because at that moment I realized that I didn't want to lose him. I realized that I loved him. So I said to him, "I love you Mike. I don't want to lose you." And I didn't lose him.

He told his family all about me but I hadn't told mine yet, especially the girls. I didn't even tell them I was dating. They were first in my life. I felt like I was betraying them to date and love a man. But I finally told them that I was dating Mike. My two oldest didn't take the news very well but my youngest daughter was elated.

It was January 28, 2000. Mike took me on a date to a fancy steakhouse for dinner. We had our own private booth. I love prime rib, and he knew it, so we both ordered prime rib and had a delicious meal. During dinner, he left to go to the restroom, or so I thought. He had actually gone back to the kitchen to talk to the waiter to ask if he would put an engagement ring on top of a cheesecake before serving dessert. The waiter was nervous about being entrusted with the ring. Mike trusted him (with eyewitnesses). So after dinner the waiter asked me, "Would you like dessert?"

I said, "Yes, what do you have?"

The waiter responded, "Apple pie, carrot cake, ice cream, and cheeeeese cake."

"Mike and I will split the cheesecake," I said.

So while Mike was talking to me romantically telling me how much he loved me, out came the cheesecake with a sparkling sapphire (my birthstone) and diamond ring on top. I took a double take. I turned to Mike, he took the ring, put it on my finger and asked, "Will you marry me?" Of course I said yes! All the waiters and waitresses were buzzing around our booth knowing that Mike was proposing to me. They all had big smiles. I was blushing and felt overjoyed.

We were married June 24, 2000. Mike was from a large family, one of ten children, and the church was full of Rubadues. We had many friends attend. Two of my girls were junior bridesmaids. My brother, Mark, gave me away. The ceremony was beautiful. The reception was so much fun with dancing under a disco ball and good food. I had never been so happy.

I had love and respect. No more abuse. The past was behind me. When I was around Mike the past didn't haunt me. It didn't hurt. I felt so good.

Two of my three daughters struggled with my new marriage. After all, they had also suffered from my two failed marriages and the abuse. It took a while for them to warm up to Mike. Mike on the other hand treated my girls as his own. They weren't his *step*daughters, they were his *daughters*. But still, he was thrown into a stepfather's role. When Mike would discipline the girls, we would hear the typical response of a stepchild, "You're not my real dad."

When we married, the girls were eleven, thirteen, and fifteen. Not easy years. There were trials and tribulations in raising them as is often the case in raising teenagers. But we got through it. All the girls learned to love him. They knew their mom was happy. They saw how a man should treat his wife – respectfully and lovingly. They saw how he adored me and how I adored him. They saw what a good man he was.

MIKE AND I HAD COMMON interests and two of them were camping and fishing. We both loved the outdoors. We fished at various lakes around Colorado. Along the shore, we would place our poles in pole holders with bells hung at the tips of the poles, and every time the bell would jingle from a bite I'd excitedly hop up and grab the pole, even if it was his. Often I would reel in the fish on his line screaming with delight. Then I'd say, "Sorry. That was your pole." And he would laugh and say, "You're so much fun to watch, it's more fun than reeling it in myself."

A favorite lake we camped and fished at had an abundance of wildlife – geese, ducks, eagles and hawks, badgers, owls, and even seagulls. (I thought, "They're lost! Don't seagulls only live near the ocean?") We admired the magnificent Rocky Mountains in the distance, and watched beautiful sunrises and sunsets. We would have a crackling fire at night and roast bratwurst for dinner, or the trout we caught if we were lucky. I loved nature, the water, and fishing as a child, and it carried over into my adulthood.

We also enjoyed going on motorcycle rides. Mike had been riding a bike for many years. When we first got married he wanted a new motorcycle, and for me to ride along. But I was afraid to get on one. I didn't think they were very safe. I also thought the backseat was so uncomfortable for the passenger. He said, "We're going to buy a bike that's comfortable for you. When we look at bikes, you try out the backseat. When you find one you like, that's the one we'll get." We ended up getting a Kawasaki Vulcan Nomad – a big bike with a very comfortable backseat. I found that Mike was a good driver and I felt safe with him. We would take trips up winding roads through the Rocky Mountains, or through backroads down in the plains.

Mike, the girls and I took frequent road trips to California, visiting my mom and friends in Santa Barbara, and his family in southern California. He loved to drive, but he always wanted to drive straight through even though it was a seventeen-hour drive from our home in Colorado to Santa Barbara. After a few trips, the girls and I finally convinced him to stay overnight in a hotel halfway to our destination. "Okay.

As long as you're happy, I'm happy," he said. As a family, we had many enjoyable, memorable times on those excursions, and what a better place to visit than Santa Barbara!

Mike also introduced me to garage sales. He always found what we needed, which I thought was amazing. One time I wanted to host a fondue party but didn't have a fondue set. He said, "I'll find one." I said, "You're kidding. You're going to find a fondue set at a garage sale?" And sure enough he did. He loved to buy fishing poles. I would find anything from nice knick-knacks for home decoration to technical books for work. It became our favorite pastime to go to garage sales on Saturday mornings during the spring and summer months.

Mike didn't have a college degree, although he was just short of earning an associate's degree in mechanics. Unlike my other husbands, it didn't intimidate him at all that I had a bachelor's in engineering. He was proud of me. Mike worked at a family business that his dad started, and many other members of his family worked there as well. It was a wire business with a production line. Mike designed almost every piece of equipment on the floor, which he also maintained and repaired. He literally wore a blue-collar one-piece outfit and came home with his clothes and hands dirtied with grease. He would call himself a blue-collar worker but I'd say, "No you're not, you're part owner of the business and you helped design the equipment with your AutoCAD software. That makes you white-collar." He told me,

"You know, there's nothing wrong with being a blue-collar worker. They are what make the world go around. We need the plumbers, electricians, auto-mechanics, carpenters, construction workers, truck drivers, and welders." He was right, but I still felt it was important for my daughters to get college degrees and encouraged them to do so, like my parents encouraged me.

When my youngest daughter was close to graduating from high school, she didn't know what she wanted to do with her life. "Hey," Mike said, "you can make good money being a refrigerator repair girl!"

I laughed out loud, "Mike, you're joking, right?"

No, he was serious.

Mike would joke that I was a snobbish white-collar worker, but he was never mean about it. And I thought Mike was one of the most intelligent men I had ever met. He was an avid reader with an incredible, extensive vocabulary. And he was usually the one helping the girls with their homework. (He was also more patient than I was.)

Mike absolutely spoiled me to death. I disliked grocery shopping but Mike liked it, so he did all the grocery shopping, always looking for the bargains. He liked to cook and usually made dinner. He helped with the chores around the house like doing the laundry and cleaning the bathrooms (which I hated and still do). I used to say to Mike, "You spoil me, and I love it."

He would reply, "You were long overdue. You deserve it. But it doesn't take away your competence.

You are a very capable person." In addition, he was a brilliant auto-mechanic and between our cars and our kids' cars, he seemed to be spending every weekend working on someone's car.

Mike loved to volunteer for the common good. For instance, once a month on Sunday mornings he would join others to serve a pancake breakfast to our church congregation. Together we cooked and served meals for the homeless at a homeless shelter. He joined a group of men called "Helping Hands" who helped out widows needing house repairs. Whenever a volunteer was needed, Mike would jump to the task.

At work, when he was in a position of hiring employees, he would interview and hire down-and-out people from the local halfway house to give them a second chance in life. He picked up hitchhikers, although I didn't like it when I was in the car with him. He always stopped to help when someone had a broken-down car alongside the road. Mike was a selfless man who went out of his way for anyone and always put other people first. People used to call him the Good Samaritan.

I believe our marriage was made in heaven. Besides the great love we had for each other, there was respect, and that was important to me. If we had a disagreement, which wasn't often, we talked to each other considerately, never trying to hurt the other, and never yelling. Mike never put me down, which was a respect I never got before.

Yes, Mike was a remarkable man, with a jolly laugh who made everyone around him laugh. I believe he was sent to me directly from God. After what I had been through in my life, he was my savior, and I really don't know where I would be today without him. And yet he would say the same to me. He said God brought me into his life and he had never been happier. I could hardly believe it was true, but it warmed my heart.

«Chapter 25»

IT WAS EARLY SPRING OF 2003. The phone rang and I answered. It was my dad. It had been a long time since I had talked to him. "Hi Dad. What's up?" I asked.

He responded, "Trink, I'm calling with bad news. I have cancer. I don't have long to live."

I was speechless. All I could say was, "Dad, I'm sorry. I don't know what to say."

He said, "How about 'I love you'."

I forced it, but I said, "I love you Dad."

When my sister, Liz, heard of his terminal cancer, she flew back to California from her home in Virginia to be with him. Up to this time, Dad had been an atheist. But Liz told me while she was back there that he wanted to be baptized. So, a pastor was called to his home since he was too weak to get out of bed, and baptized him. Then he accepted Jesus into his heart.

A couple of weeks later, Mike and I visited him at the hospice center in California, along with my two brothers. I could tell he was a changed man. Dad said to me, "When you were about two years old, we had guests over at the house and it was time to put you into bed. You didn't want to go to bed and threw a tantrum. I picked you up and took you to your room. I then hung you upside down, grabbing you by the heels, and swung you into a door with a mirror hung on it. The mirror cracked and your head was bleeding. I told your mom and the guests that you fell. Do you remember that?"

"No," I replied.

He said he was sure I remembered a lot of things he did in my childhood. Then he broke down and cried and asked for God's forgiveness and my forgiveness.

"I forgive you, Dad," I said. And I meant it.

He died on May 27, 2003 at age seventy-seven and I know he is with God in heaven.

IN THE FALL OF 2005, it was Mom's seventy-fifth birthday. It was celebrated at a park in Santa Barbara with most all of her siblings, children, grandchildren, nieces, nephews, and good friends. Mike and I attended, along with my three daughters. Her birthday was combined with a family reunion. Our family is large and I am the oldest of thirty cousins. It was a jubilant day and Mom was overjoyed to have her family and friends there to celebrate.

The next day Mom, who was living in a rest home at the time, was not feeling well. It turned out she was having problems with her stomach due to a hiatal hernia. Mom developed the hernia in her early years and had two surgeries to correct it. After the last one she almost died from complications. Apparently, her most recent operation was not a success and her hernia was causing difficulties again the day after her birthday party.

After examination, the doctors found that her stomach was in such bad shape that they had to insert a feeding tube. Mom couldn't eat or drink and was confined to bed. This would go on for five years. It was a terrible way to live.

During those five years, Mike and I and the girls would take frequent road trips to go visit her. Mike was so good to her and Mom adored Mike. Mom was so happy for me for finally having a good man in my life and being happily married.

In December 2010, Mom developed a serious infection of the colon and wasn't expected to live. While she was in the hospital, my family and I were able to visit her and say our final goodbyes. A few days later she passed away. She was eighty years old.

The loss I felt when she died was different from my dad's. What impacted me most is that no matter what resentments I had toward her, she was still my mom. And her death made me aware of the finality of life – that we are all going to die. Mom wasn't a mentally stable person and I don't think it was her fault.

Mom was a devout Catholic until the very end. Even though she wasn't able to eat and drink during her last five years on the feeding tube, a priest would still visit her once a week and give her Holy Communion. She was able to digest the Host without getting sick. I see that as a blessing from God. I believe she is now in heaven and free from pain.

«Chapter 26»

EVEN THOUGH I CONTINUED TO take my medications for bipolar II disorder, I still had trouble admitting that I was bipolar. While being married to Mike I was so happy, so happy that I didn't think I needed to take the medications anymore. I thought my mood swings were due to the difficult circumstances that I had endured before meeting Mike and not due to being bipolar.

It was also hard for me to "depend" on drugs because that's what my mom did. She abused them and couldn't live without them. I didn't want that.

In addition, one of the medications caused weight gain and I hated it. I am 5'4 ¾" tall. All my life I always weighed less than 115 pounds until I was put on these medications. I gained twenty pounds. Now 135 pounds isn't what you call really overweight but I was unhappy with my body nevertheless. Mike used to say, "You're beautiful. You're not overweight. You look great." But I didn't feel like it. So now and then I would stop taking my medications without telling anyone, including my doctor.

One time when I was off of them, Mike asked me with suspicion and concern, "Are you off your medications?" I lied and said no. "Are you sure?" he asked.

"I haven't stopped taking them," I said. But I was having mood swings, alternating between depression and irritability. I noticed and Mike noticed.

A few days later Mike said, "The pharmacist at the drugstore told me you haven't been renewing your prescriptions. You aren't taking them, are you?" I finally admitted that I wasn't.

Suddenly I had the realization – "It is true. I am bipolar." I knew it because I was happy with my life yet I was still getting depressed and having mood swings. Yes, our teenage girls could give us grief; yes my job could give me grief also, but that wasn't it. I really did have a brain chemical imbalance.

Mike went with me to an appointment with my psychiatrist to talk about it. I told him about my admission and acceptance of being bipolar, but I also told him I hated the weight gain. Fortunately, there was a new drug on the market that didn't cause weight gain that could substitute for the one I was taking. I changed over to the new medication and lost weight. I was happy.

I agree with my doctor's opinion that alcoholism is caused by a brain chemical imbalance, and I believe my mom's illness was caused by it as well. I do agree that I inherited it although mine has manifested itself in a different way. A person with a bipolar condition doesn't need a parent (or another relative) with a bipolar condition to inherit it from, and psychosis doesn't necessarily breed psychosis. It's the brain chemical imbalance that's inherited, not the condition. That's the theory as I understand it.

I see my psychiatrist at least every six months because it is required in order for him to prescribe and maintain my medications. To this day, I continue to take my medications and they are succeeding in keeping me on an even keel. That's not to say I haven't had bouts of depression a few times, which are few and far between.

After one bout of depression, I asked my doctor "Is this because I'm bipolar?"

He said, "I don't think so because you're taking your medications. I think it's because of your childhood. You've dealt with abandonment and abuse. When you are in a circumstance where you feel abandoned or abused, I think that's what brings on your depression."

That was very insightful to me. We who have had dysfunctional childhoods tend to repeat the past, especially in our relationships. Our scars don't go away, but they can heal. I am sure there is probably even more healing I can do that could improve some of my relationships.

One more note about admitting I have bipolar II disorder. There is still a great stigma associated with mental illness and it causes shame in the individual who suffers from it. Individuals with bipolar disorder are often portrayed as "crazy" in the media and even in hospitals, and are often associated with mass murderers. I have heard people use the term loosely describing, for example, a boss or acquaintance with erratic behavior or a short temper and blurt out, "He must be bipolar."

In my opinion, society hasn't progressed very far in overcoming the stigmas attached with mental illness.

People can easily admit that they suffer from depression with no shame. Depression seems to be an acceptable condition and is even common in our society. Primary care physicians readily prescribe antidepressants and people have no problem admitting they take them. The same goes for taking Valium for anxiety. But mention that you're bipolar and some people will say, "I knew there was something not quite right about her."

I believe people need to be more educated about mental illness and be less discriminating against those who suffer from it. I know that some in the mental health profession and even those on the political forefront are trying to raise awareness about mental illness, conducting workshops and speaking in public forums, with the goal to educate people and remove the stigma. However, I think there is still a long way to go.

«Chapter 27»

Throughout my ups and downs in life, I had been able to maintain a career in software engineering since graduating from college. I have twenty-eight years of experience and am retired now. I worked in a male dominated field and especially in the early years, I experienced sexual harassment before strict laws were put in place, and sex discrimination. I never broke the glass ceiling. I was passed up for promotions. I never felt as smart as the other engineers but that wasn't because I wasn't, as I later realized. At my last place of work, there were still few women engineers. I survived the layoffs during the economic downturn in 2007 and 2008; however, I sometimes wonder if I survived because they needed to meet their quota of females in the workplace.

During that economic downturn, I decided I needed to have a back-up skill in case I did get laid off, so I went back to school majoring in accounting. After three years in school while working full-time, I earned an associate of science degree in accounting. Once I left my job in engineering in 2011 (for various reasons), I worked full-time at an accounting firm preparing taxes. It was far less pay and I was working with the general public, with whom I hadn't had experience while working as an engineer. But I was proud of myself for pushing the envelope and I enjoyed the job. I wasn't discriminated against and felt like an equal with my co-workers, as there were more women in the field.

Unfortunately my job at the accounting firm came to an abrupt halt.

«Chapter 28»

IT WAS JANUARY, 2012. Mike started choking and gagging on his food. He went to his primary care physician who referred him to an ear, nose, and throat specialist. The ENT recommended an endoscopy, so on February 7, 2012 Mike went in to have the outpatient procedure.

After his procedure, I was called into the recovery room where Mike had not yet awakened from the anesthetic. The nurse said to me, "The surgeon would like to speak to you."

I had never met the doctor. Soon he came into the room, introduced himself and said, "I'm afraid I have bad news. Your husband has a malignant tumor." I was shocked and was hoping he was joking. But he wasn't. I felt my world had just turned upside down. Mike awoke and I went over to him and rubbed his head and said, "We'll get through this. They found a malignant tumor."

"Oh God," Mike said.

During the next few weeks, there were many doctor appointments with two different oncologists, one for a second opinion. The oncologist we saw for the second opinion said his cancer was in stage IV, terminal, and was incurable. He said the cancer, which was esophageal cancer, had metastasized. He said he would treat him just to make him comfortable. We could not accept that so we went back to the first oncologist. He said it was debatable whether it had metastasized and he would treat it as curable. However, he said his chances for survival were less than ten percent and as low as three percent for this type of cancer because even if treatment was successful, it always came back. We were devastated.

At this point, I realized that we had a long road ahead of us to fight the cancer. Mike needed me. So I quit my job in order to be there for him.

Mike's journey began with many outpatient procedures. He had a stent put into his esophagus to help with swallowing, which soon fell through to his stomach. He had a port put in his chest for his chemo treatments, a CAT scan, a PET scan, and a EUS (Endoscopic Ultrasonography). Then he had five weeks of chemo and radiation and was in the hospital twice for twelve days within a fourteen-day period. The first time was for a blood infection, and the second time he was in ICU with extremely low blood pressure from an allergic reaction to one of the chemo drugs. Overall, he did well during and after treatment. He experienced a few bouts of nausea but a lot of fatigue. He lost eighteen pounds.

It was a roller coaster ride of emotions. When we first got the diagnosis, I was already grieving. They call it anticipatory grief. I had days where I felt physically ill with a dagger in my heart. I curled up in bed and could only imagine Mike not being there next to me ever again and me being all alone. It was so unreal. I looked back before the diagnosis and life seemed so blissful – the bliss of ignorance. I grieved over what we had lost – our "normal" lives, good health, and dreams of living to a ripe old age together. There was an Asian couple who looked to be about in their nineties who took walks in our neighborhood, holding hands. When I watched them I thought, "That will never be us."

I kept a journal during our cancer journey. One day I wrote:

> *"I don't want to go on living if he dies. He is my best friend and I need him so much. He has always been the one to encourage me, help me with self-confidence, love me, respect me, hold me up when I'm down, make jokes and make me laugh. Life will be so empty and lonely without him. I will be so unhappy. I know I have my daughters and grandchildren and more on the way, but this is my husband. He is my companion and lover. Mike says he sees me remarrying, or tells me not to rule it out anyway. Married a fourth time? And someone to replace Mike? No. There's no one out there like Mike. He is the best man for me and a great man. I can't imagine ever being in love with anyone else.*
>
> *I'm fifty-seven and that really isn't that old. So if I live to be ninety, that's a lot of years alone. Mike says to play the piano for*

people and share my gift. He says to be a volunteer because rarely do people criticize volunteers. They appreciate them. And I need appreciation.

I need Mike."

At night I didn't sleep well. My heart hurt – real physical hurt. My body was in anguish. I hugged Mike in bed next to me and held him tight. I listened to his snoring and didn't want it to go away.

From the beginning of Mike's treatment in March, the radiologist was less optimistic than the oncologist about his prognosis. She was concerned about a suspicious spot found on his lung. She said he could have as little as three months to live, the average being nine months for esophageal cancer depending how advanced it was. The oncologist thought Mike could live another nine months but didn't think he'd live longer than one and a half years.

Mike asked the oncologist about dying – how his body would behave as he dies. The oncologist said that he would slowly lose his appetite and would be weakened to the point of losing his independence. Mike would be unable to care for himself. He said at that point hospice would be involved.

Mike and I were trying to prepare ourselves for him dying as soon as three months. We planned visits with the family and many out-of-towners came to visit. We got our wills and paperwork in order. He even showed me his filing system. We cleaned out our basement and garage of unnecessary items in addition to cleaning out our desks. He sold his motorcycle and the motorhome. He even bought me a new car so that I wouldn't have to deal with maintaining and repairing our old one and having to sell it on my own someday. We thought of everything. We faced his fate head on.

A few weeks had passed, and I wrote this entry into my journal on June 7, 2012:

> *"'And after you have suffered for a little while, the God of all grace, who has called you to his eternal glory in Christ, will himself restore, support, strengthen, and establish you.' (1 Peter 5:7-10 ESV)*
>
> *Why will I have to suffer again? I suffered enough in the past. Mike brought me total happiness. I never thought I'd suffer again. I'm scared. Why, God?"*

One day Mike had to fill out a patient questionnaire. One of the questions was, "Do you ever feel blue and depressed?" He answered yes. I felt sad and surprised because Mike maintained his optimism, yet I shouldn't have been surprised. He didn't show these feelings of depression to me. Mike said he hid them from me because I had enough sadness, anxiety, and grief going on as it was. He didn't want to add to it and give me more than I could handle. Mike was that kind of guy, always putting others before himself.

During the time of Mike's treatments, my two older daughters got engaged and wasted no time getting married. One daughter got married in June and the other in July, the same year of Mike's diagnosis. Mike gave them both away along with their biological father. With each of the weddings, the father-daughter dance was the most moving part of the wedding. There wasn't a dry eye in the place.

Mike was still alive for Christmas 2012. I thought, "What kind of presents do you get for someone who's dying?" A friend suggested that instead of waiting to pay tribute to him after he died, to give him writings and gifts of tributes before he died. So one daughter made a family video, another put together a book of memories with writings and pictures, and I wrote him a letter. Here are excerpts of what I wrote:

"Mike my true love,
This is my Christmas gift to you – to let you know what a difference you have made in my life and how you have blessed me and others – and much more.

... What I love about you so much is when you did find out a lot about my past, you still accepted me and didn't judge me. You didn't look at me as all messed up and you didn't play any games. You took me as is and saw the good in me and helped me to feel lovable.

That's how you make me feel – lovable. Because you love me no matter what.

... So we got married on June 24, 2000, and lived happily ever after, right? Well it's true, you've made me the happiest person in my whole life. And we do have a wonderful marriage. And you say I've made you happy too. But – there were the teenagers. Three more teenagers for you. It's amazing you would marry me with three teenagers to raise already knowing what it was like after your two. I look back on those years and as I've said to you many times, 'I don't know how I would have done it without you as a single parent.' And you say, 'You'd do just fine.' As you say now – 'you'll do just fine.'

But, despite the stressful times raising teenage girls our marriage held strong, not to say there weren't good times. You had your hands tied behind your back being the stepdad. I was no help to that. But you have to know that you're the best example of a stepdad there is. To you, the girls are as much your own children as the children you fathered. The girls know it. You have set an example of what a good father, and a husband, should be. They know how to be treated right. I couldn't have provided that for them on my own. Take some credit. I really couldn't have done it without you.

Thinking about our marriage, I'd like to quote the bible, 1 Corinthians 13:4-8a. 'Love is patient, love is kind. It does not envy, it does not boast, it is not proud. It is not rude, it's not self-seeking, it is not easily angered, it keeps no record of wrongs. Love does not delight in evil but rejoices with the truth. It always protects, always trusts, always hopes, always perseveres. Love never fails.'

Isn't this so true about us? And so true about you! You're patient, kind, you do not envy, do not boast. You're not proud, not rude, not self-seeking, not easily angered, and you do not keep record of wrongs. You do not delight in evil but rejoice in the truth. You always protect, trust, hope, and persevere. I am so fortunate to have you. I am so blessed to know true love. You have provided that for me. You've given me respect, and you spoil me to death and I love it. I never had much respect before I met you so I didn't respect myself. You gave me self-respect.

Isn't it cool how we're so in tune to each other? When I say something, you know what I mean and can finish the sentence. We think alike (well, most of the time). Sometimes I say what you were going to say or vice versa. You're in tune with my feelings. Sometimes I think you're more in tune with them than I am. I get confused and you help me sort things out. You understand me. You KNOW me. And you accept me. You encourage me. You root me on.

You've taught me to 'Don't sweat the small stuff', although I still need to practice it. I must not take life so seriously. You bring so much laughter into my life. You laugh a lot and you're so great at cheering people up, especially me and your children. I need to laugh more.

You've taught me to believe in myself – that I have a good heart. I am determined and can do almost anything I set my mind on. I persevere. I'm not a quitter. I need to keep reminding myself of that, especially with times to come. You've always said I am gentle but I can't be walked on. You taught me to realize that I will no longer allow people to disrespect me or abuse me. I am realizing that I am intelligent after all, and people enjoy my music and my talent, even if I'm not a concert pianist. You're my biggest fan and have encouraged me to volunteer to play the piano for others and keep playing for myself also.

You've taught me that I need to 'let go' of the girls. They're all grown up now. I must listen to them and not force my advice or opinions on them. It takes practice but I'm making an effort. I'm learning to put them in God's hands. But I still wonder what they'll do without your shoulder to cry on, without your wisdom, without your optimism, without your strength. I hope I'll be enough for them.

You'll always be known as the Good Samaritan. You always put others before yourself and you'd lay down your life for others. You risked your life for the man who was on fire from the accident in California. And you don't boast. You do little acts of kindness every day, like putting the grocery carts away, pulling over to help someone with their car broken down alongside the road. You started the Social Committee for the HOA and the neighborhood is better off because of it – neighbors getting to know neighbors, less complaints.

I love the story you've told about the priest asking the classroom what they wanted to be when they grow up. You said everyone

laughed when you said, 'a good husband and father'. And the priest said that it was the most honorable thing to aspire to. You know what? – you have been the best husband to me and father to your children that there could be (and you raised nieces and nephews too). Your dream has come true. I think God is proud of you.
I love you so much."

What a special Christmas that was. Mike was choked up with tears. We all were.

After Christmas, I could tell Mike's health was declining. He was getting weaker.

On February 25, 2013, I entered into my journal:

"So my feelings ... this is the imagery I have ... I'm standing at a doorway, peering into darkness ahead. It's full of pain and suffering, loneliness, and like death, only I know I wouldn't die if I walked through it. I would have to live through it. I see an opening on the other side, but it's very far away. I know I can't avoid walking through this darkness. I must go there. I know I can't compare myself to Jesus, but I feel like Him when he prayed to God, 'My Father, if it is possible, may this cup be taken from me. Yet not as I will, but as you will.' He knew what pain and suffering he had to face. I

face it with dread and it affects me physically."

March 7, 2013 was another fateful day. After several trips to the ER and admission into the hospital where Mike ended up having a spinal tap, the doctors discovered that his cancer had metastasized to his spinal fluid. The doctor said he had just weeks to live. The oncologist told Mike that he could choose to have radiation of the brain and injections of chemo into the spinal fluid to extend his life, but he said the odds of the treatment working were very low. He also said it would lower his quality of life. Mike wanted to go on with the treatment. He later told me, "I'm not going down without a fight."

Because the cancer had gotten into his spinal fluid and was starting to affect his brain, Mike had to stop driving and I was told not to leave him alone for long periods of time. The hardest thing for Mike was to be robbed of his independence.

On March 9, Mike wrote an email to his family and friends explaining his condition. Mike had a good attitude as can be seen in the last paragraph of his email:

"I'm still doing well at this time. God has blessed me with this year. I will have seen three of my daughters married, I've had reasonably good health and a real blessed year. I still have time left on this earth and

intend to enjoy it. Unfortunately, I am not allowed to travel so I can't get out to see any of you. But come down here and we may catch a fish together or at least tell some tall tales.
Love you all,
Mike"

Mike had always been at peace with dying ever since the day he was diagnosed with cancer. He was not afraid of dying and knew he was going to heaven, knew he'd be with God, and that it would be wonderful.

Mike's daughter from his previous marriage got married on April 7, 2013. Mike walked her down the aisle even though he could hardly walk from being so physically weak. He barely made it through the father-daughter dance. Like the two other weddings when he danced with my daughters, there wasn't a dry eye in the place. The whole Rubadue family attended – which included his mother and all nine siblings. We all knew that his time was near.

After the wedding, a little over a week later, Mike and I were sitting on the edge of the bed and he wanted to pray. It went something like this:

"Dear God,
Show us how we can show our thankfulness to you. Show us how to be grateful for all the things you have done for us. Help us to continue to do for others. And God, I don't

think I have a lot of time left. I've tried to take care of Kate and get everything ready for her, but if I've missed anything, please let me know. I love her very much. And I love our kids very much and I know they love me. Show me what to do next God. Show me what to do next.
Amen."

The following morning he told me he realized that he was getting more limited, "which is a pain in the butt," he said. He said he didn't feel like starting a new book to read, and he loved to read. He said he lacked motivation to do anything. He liked to watch T.V. but he said he no longer liked most of the shows because they had so much yelling and screaming and people were saying bad things.

He said that on so many levels – physical, emotional, and mental, he had no motivation. He said most of his lack of motivation was due to the pain. He had a new pain on the left side of his back. He had terrible hiccups (we never knew the cause) that were constant and were wrenching his stomach. But he said that he was not afraid. He said God had blessed him in every way with everything he had ever asked for. He said our youngest daughter wasn't married yet but he was sure she would be someday, and "that's way cool." He didn't feel bad that he wasn't going to be there for her wedding, as he was there for all the other girls. "She knows I love her."

He said he didn't know when he would cross the line to want to go, to leave us. He knew we all wanted him to stay. He knew he would make his daughter's wedding. Now that that was over, he didn't know how long he would stay with us. He said the pain he was in was worsening his quality of life. He said if he were totally functional it wouldn't be an issue.

Mike told me that for the past week he had been having the same dream about Jesus. He said he saw Jesus's face smiling at him, reaching his hand out to him. Mike tried to reach back but his hands would go through a handcuff, or sometimes a tube, and their fingers couldn't touch. But he said it was still a happy dream because Jesus was smiling at him and he was in the presence of Jesus.

Then one night when Mike was dozing in and out of sleep, he told me that he saw Jesus's face again and He was smiling and "had a sense of humor." Mike laughed and said, "It's good that Jesus has a sense of humor." I started laughing too.

"It's good to hear you laugh." Mike said. "That's good."

It was time for Mike to be under hospice care which we agreed would be in our home. A hospital bed was brought into our family room. Mike could no longer sit up.

On April 16, 2013, I entered the following into my journal:

"The time is near I think. I can't believe this is really happening. I know I have to let go at some point and let him know that it's okay for him to go and that I'll be all right. But deep down, I don't want to let go. My friend said that he probably sense my feelings. He can't let go peacefully until I let go. She said someday I'll get to the point where I don't want him to be suffering so much from pain, then I'll feel in my heart that it's time to let him go and be with Jesus in no pain."

Mike suffered a lot during the last week of his life. It wasn't pretty. Mike eventually stopped eating and became less lucid. But one day he opened his eyes and exclaimed, "We should believe in God and tell others about Him. We should not lie and cheat and steal. The power of the Holy Spirit!"

On April 19, I summoned a Catholic priest to give Mike his last rites. Mike was fairly lucid and prayed the Our Father and Hail Mary with him. The priest said to Mike, "Do not be afraid," and Mike answered that he was not. As the priest was leaving, he told me that it would be a more peaceful passing for Mike if I told him I was ready to let him go and that he would be with Jesus and I would be okay. So I went to Mike's bedside and while he was sleeping, I whispered in his ear that it was okay to go … that I'd be okay. Then

Mike woke up, put his arm around me and said he loved me, and fell asleep again.

After a fourteen-month battle with cancer, Mike passed away on the morning of April 28, 2013. Three of our daughters were at his side when he died. I was holding his hand when he took his last breath. He was sixty-one years old.

«Chapter 29»

GRIEF. A NEW STAGE OF MY LIFE. At this writing, it has been five years and ninth months since Mike died. Most people who haven't lost a loved one think that after a year your grieving should be over. You should be "moving on."

You don't move on or move *through*, as if there's another side to reach. You live with it, always. It becomes a part of you. You are never the same person again. Whether you like it or not, you change. Life has been turned upside down and will never be the same again.

In the first few days and weeks after Mike died, just small tasks were an effort, like making coffee (for only one), cooking dinner (for only one), and grocery shopping (for only one), even pumping gas and taking out the trash.

Then there were the bigger tasks to handle, like having the car and house repaired and maintained.

My daughters, of course, grieved too. The family dynamics were out of balance. The strong shoulder to cry on was no longer with us. I knew I couldn't fill Mike's shoes and felt bad about it. I almost felt resentment from the girls that I couldn't be like him – he the optimist, me the pessimist.

A few months after Mike passed away, I wrote in my journal:

"I am now half of a whole. Mike and I complemented each other, completed each other. Now I'm incomplete. I seek wholeness again. But how do I do that? I can't be both introvert and extrovert. I can't be both the quiet type and the gregarious, jovial, social type. I can't be both Mom and Dad. I'm finding that out. I can't be Mike.

It was "we". Now it's "I".

It was "ours". Now it's "mine".

We were a couple. Now I'm an individual.

We were together. Now I'm alone.

When I fell down, he picked me up.

When I was sad, he made me laugh.

Mike was my protector and defender. Now I'm vulnerable.

He saw the best in me. I'm everything I am today because he loved me. I've come so far.

Mike knew me like no other. There will not be another who can know me like Mike did.

With Mike my life had meaning. Now I question it, yet seek it.

Mike was my mirror. It reflected who I was with him. It affirmed me as a lovable, valuable, worthy person. Now I look at the mirror on the wall. I see sadness. I want to be who I was when I was with him. I don't want a new me. I don't want a new identity. But change has been forced upon me. Life is different, and I know I will change because of it.

There's a void in our family which has put things out of balance. His role is unfulfilled — the father, the husband, the counselor, the rock. I can't meet expectations. They can't meet mine.

Unresolved issues in my past have been resurrected – abandonment, mistreatment, criticism, disrespect, belittlement, instability – I thought they had been resolved.

Must I resolve them now and reopen the wounds, when my new wound is so great? Must this be part of the grief journey? Old pain and new pain. It overwhelms me. With Mike there was no pain. The memories didn't matter because he was there. The memories had no pain because he was there. He made me happy.

Life goes on, and with it new stressors and disappointments that heighten his loss and deepen my grief. Mike would have been there with his optimism, encouragement, hope, and comfort. Now I must cope without him. But thank God for friends and kinship with others who have also lost a spouse and understand my pain.

But there are little rays of sunlight that peek through the dark clouds. A newborn. Grandchildren. They bring me moments of joy. Their giggling. Their unbridled enthusiasm. Their wonderment in the little things of life. Their affection and hugs – something I don't get daily anymore.

And another thing that brings me momentary joy – sharing my music with others. Mastering a difficult piece of music. Creativity. It's part of me. It's part of who I am.

But it's not all of who I am, and I wonder how I'll ever be whole again and what that wholeness looks like, because it will be a different kind of wholeness, not what it was."

It is that wholeness I continue to seek, and after these years and months since Mike has died, I *am* becoming whole again. But it is the foundation that Mike laid for me that has helped me from falling apart.

About six months after Mike was diagnosed with terminal cancer, I asked him if he could write me a love letter – something I could hold onto after he died. I expected to have a multiple page letter. He wrote me this on one page:

"Do you see what I see?

A gorgeous sexy woman

Amazingly intelligent, surprisingly humble

Incredibly talented pianist and artist

A lady with lots of love in her heart

Passionate, determined, a do it person

A finisher, not a quitter

A true Christian in every way

A wonderful lady with a smile and laugh to warm my heart

A gentle lady

The woman I love"

He told me to tape it on the mirror and read it every morning. I followed through and to this day it is still on my mirror.

Another thing I asked Mike to do before he died was to make a video tape of him for me to keep and cherish – a sort of verbal love letter with words of encouragement to help me go on after he left us, and reminiscing about our lives together, including the children. He did make that video, with me filming, and it is long – about an hour and a half. It is a treasure which I have watched many times after his passing.

He started out telling the story of how God led him to me, which was a real round-about way. He said I was just what he was looking for in a wife. He spoke so lovingly into the camera as I was filming. As I asked of him, he gave me many words of encouragement and parting words of wisdom.

He told me not to forget that I am a lovable, valuable person. He said to me, "If anyone tells you otherwise, DISMISS them. And I believe that you now know the difference between someone who will treat you right and someone who won't."

"What if I regress? How will I stop from regressing?" I asked.

In summary he said, "You won't let yourself go there anymore. You are stronger than you believe. You have God, you, and your family. I believe that the angels will wrap their arms around you and comfort and protect you. And I believe that your family won't let you down. You need to keep being a mom and a grandma. You can't let them down. They will be watching you on how you are handling your life after I pass. You will be an example to them. And you will be having more grandkids. Kids are the best medicine. They will give you unconditional love and joy. You can't just curl up in a ball and check out. You are needed. Some days you'll get in a funk. We all do. But then you'll pick yourself back up and go on. Life can still be beautiful after I pass. You can enjoy life again. It will be different, but you can do it. I want you to enjoy life again. I NEED you to. And don't stop sharing your music with others. Your music is beautiful and brings joy to others. Keep playing. You won't be criticized like you were at work. Volunteers are appreciated, and so is your music."

Mike helped me to look in the mirror and see in myself that I AM a lovable, valuable person. Since Mike's passing, there have been a few people in my life that haven't been kind to me, and I am still a sensitive person and it affects my self-confidence and self-esteem. Those are the times when I really miss Mike's protection of me. But I'm learning to protect myself. There are days I just want to give up and be with Mike. But I remember his parting words. "I NEED you to keep going on. Your children need you."

Most importantly, I lean on God. He's been there alongside me every step of the way. I know that when I have days where I cry in grief and anguish, He is there to hold me and comfort me. He comforts me through His words. Verses like:

"God is our refuge and strength, a very present help in trouble." (Psalm 46:1 ESV)

"Blessed are those who mourn, for they shall be comforted." (Matthew 5:4 ESV)

"He heals the brokenhearted and binds up their wounds." (Psalm 147:3 ESV)

> *"But they that wait upon the Lord shall renew their strength; they shall mount up with wings as eagles; they shall run, and not be weary; and they shall walk and not faint." (Isaiah 40:31 NIV)*
>
> *"Weeping may stay for the night, but joy comes in the morning." (Psalm 30:5b WEB)*

And the one I hold close to my heart is from Jeremiah 29:11 *NIV*:

> *"For I know the plans I have for you," declares the Lord, "plans to prosper you and not to harm you, plans to give you hope and a future."*

After Mike's passing, I have grown, even though I didn't want to. I wanted everything to stay the same – the way it was with Mike. But of course that couldn't be. Now as I continue on this journey toward becoming whole again, I am making a new life for myself. I'm finding out that this new type of wholeness is different from what it was, like Mike said it would be. Mike completed me when he was here on earth. Now it is God that completes me. It's like the song that was sung at our wedding called "You Are My All In All", by Dennis Jernigan. It goes like this:

"You are my strength when I am weak
You are the treasure that I seek
You are my all in all

Seeking You as a precious jewel
Lord, to give up I'd be a fool
You are my all in all

Taking my sin, my cross, my shame
Rising up again I bless Your name
You are my all in all

When I fall down You pick me up
When I am dry You fill my cup
You are my all in all"

I'll always miss Mike. But I'm grateful that God brought him into my life. I was blessed to experience true love and respect that many people never do. I am a changed person because of him. He was my rock. But now God is my rock. I didn't think I could go on after Mike died. But along with Mike's parting words that I cherish deep in my heart, I've experienced God's mercy, comfort, compassion, love, promises, and hope, to help me carry on.

«Chapter 30»

"Praise be to...the Father of compassion and the God of all comfort, who comforts us in all our troubles, so that we can comfort those in any trouble with the comfort we ourselves receive from God."
(2 Corinthians 1:3-4 NIV)

I CAN RELATE TO THOSE who have been physically and emotionally abused, who are children of an alcoholic, who moved a lot growing up, who have lived with someone with a mental illness, who are bipolar, who have suffered a miscarriage, who have suffered abandonment, who have gone through a divorce, who are suicidal, who have been sexually violated, who have gone through a bankruptcy, who are or have been a single parent, who have dealt with cancer, who are widowed – because I have experienced all of these things.

I can choose to be held in bondage by my past mistakes and sufferings, wallowing in self–pity and despair, or I can choose to move forward and run the race God has set before me, focusing on the prize, and always remembering to be thankful for all that He has done for me in the midst of pain. I can learn from my past but not be bound to it. I can be bitter, or I can forgive. I can feel shame, or I can be purified by God's forgiveness. I choose to move forward, always be thankful, learn from my past, try to forgive others, and accept God's forgiveness.

I can't say that in remembering my past I still don't feel pain. While writing my memoir, I broke down several times as the memories were very painful, but it was also healing at the same time. I wrote down experiences I had never told anyone – family, friends, and even psychotherapists. I had to face memories that I didn't want to remember. I wanted to keep them buried. But they were still there to haunt me. Now they're out in the open. I've faced my fears, and with God's grace and comfort, I am now going to be okay.

I know that God has more good things in store for me. He has already blessed me with so much of His goodness in the past few years. After Mike died, I didn't think I could feel joy again. But I have.

God has blessed me with many grandchildren and I'm a proud Nana. I've explored new interests like sculpting and gardening. I've had the opportunity to travel and visit with family. As often as I can, I visit the seashore and commune with the ocean – which I still have a great love for. I socialize with wonderful friends, some of whom I met in my cancer support group and grief group. We have a special bond and understand each other, having gone through the same experiences. Most of all, as Mike encouraged me to do, I volunteer playing the piano at a local hospital and rest homes. I find that the music is just as therapeutic to the people I play for as it is for me. Perhaps that is God's main purpose for me. I know Mike would be proud. I have honored his wishes.

There might be more pain and suffering ahead. That's part of life. As my dad would say, "I never promised you a rose garden." But I believe that out of bad can come good, and no matter what life throws at you, God is still good. God will continue to carry me through, as He always has. Sometimes we just have to take it one step at a time.

Questions for Thought or Discussion

1. What parts of the story do you relate to?

2. What insights have you gained from reading this story?

3. Does reading this memoir inspire you to write your own, whether it's only to share with your family or also with friends and strangers?

4. Does reading this memoir encourage you to journal?

5. Do you relate to any of the parts of the diary that the author wrote in during her adolescence?

6. The author said that in writing her story she faced memories that she didn't want to remember and wanted to keep them buried. In reading this story, were you reminded of memories of your own that you wanted to keep buried?

7. Have you ever turned your back on God or feel like He has turned His back on you?

8. When in your life have you felt God's mercy?

9. Do you believe that out of bad can come good? If so, name a situation when that has happened in your life.

10. Do you believe that through the trials and hardships you have experienced, God is still good?

«Acknowledgements»

It is my daughter, Rachel, who planted the seed to write my memoir. I am grateful that she did. I intended to write my story for my daughters, but then when I began it, I realized it could reach out to a wider audience. I owe it to my daughters for loving me, supporting me, and encouraging me to share my story with others.

My sister, Liz, was of great help in validating my memories and sharing her own, providing details that I didn't remember, and offering reassurance when I hit roadblocks.

Debbie and Linda were the first to read, edit, and critique my initial draft. I am indebted to them for their time, expert editing, and suggestions.

Special thanks go out to Vicki for her thorough proofreading and editing, and for her encouraging and heartfelt words after reading about my life. She closely witnessed the journey through cancer that Mike and I took together and has buoyed me with her praise and inspiration as I grow through grief. My friend Lisa has also traveled this journey with me, and I value her insights and recommendations in reviewing my manuscript.

I thank Jerry who did a terrific job restoring a forty-year-old photo used for my book cover, and Henry for his critique on the book cover design.

I am so appreciative of my close friend, Julie, who was such a good listener and sounding board as I talked incessantly about my book and its progress. She has been a friend in whom I can confide in and trust, and has believed in me through the whole process of writing my memoir.

«About the Author»

Kate Rubadue is a graduate of the University of California Santa Barbara in electrical and computer engineering, and also holds an associate's degree in accounting. Kate is retired and lives in Northern Colorado.

Kate spends much of her time traveling and visiting her daughters and grandchildren. She enjoys gardening, fishing, and sculpting as a new hobby. Kate has experienced many special moments playing the piano as a volunteer at a local hospital and various rest homes.

Facebook.com/AGirlNamedTrink

www.ingramcontent.com/pod-product-compliance
Lightning Source LLC
Chambersburg PA
CBHW021407290426
44108CB00010B/423